Helion & Company Limited
Unit 8 Amherst Business Centre
Budbrooke Road
Warwick
CV34 5WE
England
Tel. 01926 499 619
Email: info@helion.co.uk
Website: www.helion.co.uk
Twitter: @helionbooks
Visit our blog http://blog.helion.co.uk/

Designed & typeset by Farr out Publications,
    Wokingham, Berkshire
Cover design Paul Hewitt, Battlefield Design
    (www.battlefield-design.co.uk)

Cover artwork
The front cover shows an Avro York and is
detailed in the colour section.

The rear cover artwork shows the USAF
Douglas C-47 Skytrain 293087 'Camel
Caravan to Berlin'. This aircraft was painted
specially for the special delivery of Clarence
the Camel, a present to the children of
West Berlin from the 86th Fighter Group at
Neubiberg Air Force Base, near Munich in a
USAF public relations initiative. (Artwork by
Goran Sudar)

ISBN 978-1-914059-03-2

British Library Cataloguing-in-Publication
    Data
A catalogue record for this book is available
    from the British Library

We always welcome receiving book
proposals from prospective authors.

CONTENTS

Note: In order to simplify the use of this book, all names, locations and geographic
designations are as provided in *The Times World Atlas*, or other traditionally accepted major
sources of reference, as of the time of described events.

Dedicated to my Dad, who would have been fascinated by it all.

ACKNOWLEDGEMENTS

George Jenks of the Avro Heritage Museum, Woodford; and John Evans of the Pembroke Dock Sunderland Trust, Pembroke for permission to use their images. Special thanks to the wonderful people at Cornwall Library Service who have fed my desire for knowledge for the last few years.

Thanks to Tom Cooper, Anderson Subtil, George Anderson, Luca Canossa and Goran Sudar for their expert cartographic and illustrative skills. Thanks to Albert Grandolini for help with sourcing images. Thanks to Katie for her amazing Photoshop skills. Many thanks to Tom Cooper and Andy Miles from Helion for their encouragement and constructive comments.

I would also like to thank Sara, Alex and Katie for their love, encouragement and for all the other things in life!

ABBREVIATIONS

ACC	Allied Control Commission
ADF	Automatic Direction Finder, a navigational aid
ALTF	Air Lift Task Force (USAF)
BABS	Blind Approach Beacon System
BAFO	British Air Forces of Occupation (RAF)
BAOR	British Army of the Rhine
BASC	Berlin Air Safety Centre
BCZ	Berlin Control Zone, air traffic control area
BEALCOM	Berlin Airlift Committee
BFS	British Frontier Service
BICO	Bipartite Control Office
Bizone	Free trade zone between the British and American occupation zones in post-war Germany, a.k.a. Bi-Zone or Bizonia.
BRD	Bundesrepublik Deutschland, term used by DDR to describe the Federal Republic of Germany.
BRIXMIS	The British Commander-in-Chief's Mission to the Soviet Forces of Occupation in Germany, a.k.a. 'the Mission'.
CAA	Civil Aeronautics Administration (US)
CALTF	Combined Airlift Task Force
CCG(BE)	Control Commission Germany (British Element)
CDU	Christlich Demokratische Union Deutschlands, Christian Democratic Union of Germany, centre-right West German political party
COMINFORM	Communist Information Bureau (USSR)
COMINTERN	Communist International (USSR)
CPC	Communist Party of China, led by Mao Zedong
DDR	Deutsche Demokratische Republik, German Democratic Republic/East Germany
DP	Displaced Person, normally a refugee or a released prisoner of war/forced labourer
DVdI	Deutsche Verwaltung des Innern, the East German Administration of the Interior, forerunner to MdI
DVP	Deutsche Volkspolizei, East German People's Police
EAC	European Advisory Council
EUCOM	US Army Airlift Support Command
FDJ	Freie Deutsche Jugend, Free German Youth, youth wing of the East German SED for young people between 1914 to 1943
FRG	Federal Republic of Germany, Bundesrepublik Deutschland (BRD), West Germany, a.k.a. the 'Bonn Republic'
GCA	Ground Controlled Approach, navigation aid
GDR	German Democratic Republic, East Germany
IFF	Identification Friend or Foe, transponder-based aviation identification system
IFR	Instrument Flight Rules, method of aerial navigation
KDA	Kampfgruppen der Arbeiterklasse, Combat Groups of the Working Class (factory militia)
KGB	Komitet Gosudarstvennoy Bezopasnosti, the 'Committee for State Security', the Soviet domestic and foreign secret police
KPD	Kommunistische Partei Deutschlands, the German Communist Party
KVP	Kasernierte Volkspolizei, Barracked People's Police
LDPD	Liberal-Demokratische Partei Deutschlands, the East German Liberal Democratic Party
MATS	Military Air Transport Service (USAF)
MdI	Ministerium des Innern, East German Ministry of the Interior (the former DVdI)
MGB	Ministerstvo Gosudarstvennoy Bezopasnosti, Ministry of State Security, predecessor to the KGB, 1946 to 1953
MMFL	La Mission Militaire Francaise de Liaison, the French Mission to the Soviet Occupation Forces in Germany
MTI	Moving Target Indicator, air traffic control aid
NAAFI	Navy, Army and Air Force Institutes, British military base retail shop
NATO	North Atlantic Treaty Organization
NDB	Non-Directional Beacon, navigation aid
NDPD	National-Demokratische Partei Deutschlands, the East German National Democratic Party
NKGB	Narodny Kommissariat Gosudarstvennoy Bezopasnosti, People's Directorate of State Security, predecessor to the KGB, 1943 to 1946
NKVD	Naródnyiy Komissariát Vnútrennikh Del, Soviet People's Commissariat for Internal Affairs, the

	Soviet Secret Police 1941-1943 and predecessor to the KGB
OMGUS	Office of Military Government, United States
Orbat	Order of Battle
PAP	Pierced Aluminium Planking, used for runways and roadways
POW	Prisoner of War
PPI	Planned Position Indicator, air traffic control aid
PSP	Pierced Steel Planking, used for runways and roadways
PX	Post Exchange, US Army base retail shop (BX, Base Exchange on USAF bases)
RIAS	Rundfunk im Amerikanischen Sektor, Radio In the American Sector, US propaganda radio service based in West Berlin
RMI	Radio Magnetic Indicator, navigation aid
RRS	Radio Range Station, navigation aid
SAC	Strategic Air Command (USAF)
SED	Sozialistische Einheitspartei Deutschlands; the Socialist Unity Party of Germany, East German ruling political party
SHAEF	Supreme Headquarters Allied Expeditionary Force
SMA	Soviet Military Administration in Germany, a.k.a. SMAG, SMAD (Sowjetische Militäradministration in Deutschland) and SVAG (Sovyetskaya Voyennaya Administratsya v Germanii)
SMLM	Soviet Military Liaison Mission
SOXMIS	Soviet Military Liaison Mission to the other three occupying powers in Germany.
SPD	Sozialdemokratische Partei Deutschlands, the German Socialist Social Democratic Party
Trizone	Triple free trade zone between the British, American and French occupation sectors in post-war Germany
USAFE	United States Air Force Europe
USMLM	United States Military Liaison Mission, the US Mission to the Soviet Occupation Forces in Germany
USSR	Union of Soviet Socialist Republics, the Soviet Union
VAR	Visual Aural Radio Range, navigation aid
VFR	Visual Flight Rules, method of aerial navigation
VHF	Very High Frequency, range of radio frequencies from 30 to 300 MHz
Vopo/VP	VolksPolizei, the East German 'People's' Police Force
Wehrmacht	The German armed forces during the Second World War

Timeline

Date	Event
June 1914	Assassination of Archduke Ferdinand
February 1917	Russian February Revolution
October 1917	Bolshevik October Revolution
December 1917	Russian armistice with Germany
3 March 1918	Brest-Litovsk Treaty
11 November 1918	Armistice, effective end of First World War
30 December 1918	German Communist Party (Kommunistische Partei Deutschlands or KPD) formed
2 March 1919	Comintern founded in Moscow
28 June 1919	Treaty of Versailles
30 December 1922	Soviet Union formed
21 January 1924	Lenin dies
30 January 1933	Hitler becomes German Chancellor
23 August 1939	Molotov-Ribbentrop Pact
1 September 1939	Germany invades western and southern Poland
17 September 1939	Soviet Union invades eastern Poland
3 September 1939	Great Britain declares war on Germany
2 September 1940	Destroyers for Bases agreement
11 March 1941	Lend-Lease Bill comes into effect
22 June 1941	Germany invades the Soviet Union (Operation Barbarossa)
12 July 1941	Mutual defence agreement between Great Britain and Soviet Union
9-11 August 1941	Placentia Bay Conference between Churchill and Roosevelt
7 December 1941	Japanese attack on US Naval Base Pearl Harbor
8 December 1941	US declares war on Japan

Timeline (continued)	
Date	**Event**
22 December 1941 - 14 January 1942	First Washington Conference between Churchill and Roosevelt
1 January 1942	Declaration by The United Nations
19-30 October 1943	Foreign Ministers Conference in Moscow creates European Advisory Commission (EAC)
28 November - 1 December 1943	Tehran Conference between Churchill, Roosevelt and Stalin
4-11 February 1945	Yalta Conference between Churchill, Roosevelt and Stalin
14 April 1945	FDR dies, Truman becomes US President
30 April 1945	Hitler commits suicide
2 May 1945	Ulbricht's group arrives in Berlin
8 May 1945	VE Day
13 May 1945	Berliner Rundfunk goes on air, controlled by Soviets
19 May 1945	Berlin city government re-instituted under Soviets
19 May 1945	First post-war newspaper published in Berlin (Soviet controlled)
10 June 1945	KPD re-formed
30 July 1945	Verlag Neuer Weg, the KPD's official publishing house formed
26 June 1945	United Nations Charter signed at a ceremony in San Francisco
23 June 1945	US troops make an aborted attempt to enter Berlin
4 July 1945	American and British troops finally enter the city
11 July 1945	Allied Control Council (ACC) sits for the first time
16 July 1945	Trinity Test
17 July- 2 August 1945	Potsdam Conference between Churchill (later Attlee), Truman and Stalin
26 July 1945	Clement Attlee becomes British Prime Minister
26 July 1945	French Zone of Occupation confirmed
26 July 1945	The Potsdam Declaration
29 July 1945	Japan rejected the Potsdam terms
6 August 1945	Atomic bomb dropped on Hiroshima
8 August 1945	Soviet Union declares war on Japan
9 August 1945	Atomic bomb dropped on Nagasaki
15 August 1945	VJ Day
30 November 1945	Berlin Control Zone and Air Corridors established by ACC
7 February 1946	RIAS (Radio in the American Sector) starts broadcasting
5 March 1946	Churchill's 'Sinews of Peace' speech in Fulton, Missouri
7 March 1946	Freie Deutsche Jugend (Free German Youth or FDJ) formed
21 April 1946	SED formed
23 April 1946	Neues Deutschland (or New Germany) the SED's newspaper launched
2 December 1946	Bizone agreement signed by USA and Great Britain, effective 1 January 1947
12 March 1947	Truman announces the 'Truman Doctrine'
5 June 1947	Marshall Plan announced in speech by George Marshall
22 September 1947	Cominform (Communist Information Bureau) created
19 December 1947	Truman submits European Recovery Plan a.k.a. The Marshall Plan to Congress
20 March 1948	Soviets withdraw from ACC
3 April 1948	Foreign Assistance Act (a.k.a. the European Cooperation Act, European Recovery Plan or Marshall Plan) becomes law
5 April 1948	British European Airways Viking airliner collides with a Soviet Yak fighter killing 15 people

Timeline (*continued*)	
Date	**Event**
7 June 1948	United States, United Kingdom, France and three Benelux countries issued a communique announcing the steps they were taking to begin rehabilitating Germany as a State in its own right
15 June 1948	Soviets close autobahn bridge over the River Elbe 'for repairs'
16 June 1948	Soviets also walk out of Berlin Kommandatura
18 June 1948	OMGUS press-conference announces new currency for the western zones; the Deutsche Mark or D-Mark
20 June 1948	D-Mark comes into force
20 June 1948	American military train halted at Marienborn
21 June 1948	US C-47s fly in supplies for US garrison to Tempelhof in the American sector
23 June 1948	Soviet power station stops supplying western sectors
24 June 1948	Soviets announce they are creating new currency for their zone, the Ost Mark
24 June 1948	Soviets suspend all road and barge traffic, cut off the water and electricity and halt all supplies of coal, food and milk. The blockade begins
24 June 1948	BAFO implements Operation Knicker to keep the British garrison supplied
28 June 1948	British and Americans begin supplying civilian population of Berlin as well
8 July 1948	USAF C-47 crashes, killing all three on board. First fatality of airlift
8 August 1948	First day where airlift brings in more than daily requirement
16 December 1948	Tegel becomes fully operational
27 July 1948	The first civilian contract flight took place by a Flight Refuelling Ltd Avro Lancastrian
15 October 1948	USAFE and BAFO create unified command structure, the Combined Airlift Task Force (CALTF), headed by General Tunner
9 September 1948	Huge demonstration at Platz der Republik against blockade and Soviet intimidation
4 April 1949	North Atlantic Treaty Organization (NATO) is formed
8 April 1949	France is admitted to the Bizone (Trizone)
16 April 1949	Busiest day of the airlift delivering 12,940 tons. Aircraft were landing every minute
4 May 1949	Agreement reached to lift blockades on 12 May
8 May 1949	West German Parliamentary Council in Bonn adopts 'Basic Law for the Federal Republic of Germany' allowing formation of The Federal Republic of Germany
12 May 1949	Blockade lifted
12 May 1949	Basic Law approved by Western Powers
23 May 1949	The Federal Republic of Germany comes into being
23 May 1949	Summit between former Allied powers to discuss 'German Question'. Ends on 20 June 1949 with no agreement
16 August 1949	British terminate the use of civilian contract flights
29 August 1949	Soviets successfully test their first atomic bomb
1 September 1949	CALTF is disbanded
30 September 1949	Last American flight of the airlift takes place
1 October 1949	US Airlift Task Force disbanded
1 October 1949	Mao Zedong declares the founding of the People's Republic of China (PRC)
6 October 1949	Last British flight of the airlift takes place
7 October 1949	Deutsche Demokratische Republik (DDR), German Democratic Republic created
15 October 1949	46 Group RAF return to the UK

INTRODUCTION

As the dust was still settling from the Second World War, the world powers were laying foundations for what was to become the Cold War. It was not going to be a typical war; there was no invasion, no formal declaration by belligerent governments, no blitzkrieg or area bombing. It was to be played out through competing ideologies, political manoeuvring, brinkmanship and rampant technological development, creating new existential risks for all of humanity.

Many readers will have lived through some or all of the Cold War. They may remember the times of great international crisis, the follies of Civil Defence, the intrepid escapes over (and under) the Berlin Wall, the suffocating fear of the four-minute warning and nuclear holocaust. The Cold War was *their* war, while the Second World War was perhaps their *parent's* war, and the Great War their *grandparent's* war.

In a 1948 speech, Winston Churchill, said that 'Those that fail to learn from history are condemned to repeat it.'[1] Applying that maxim, the Cold War is still highly relevant to today's society. The missile silos are still primed, the ballistic missile submarines still patrol silently, and the world's leaders still clash on the international stage. The ideologies may have changed, but the risks are still very real.

The city of Berlin found itself at the crossroads of European intrigue and conflict throughout most of the 20th century and on the front line for much of the Cold War. For more than 40 years, tales of intrigue, courage, steadfastness, deception, suffering and danger flowed from the city, and it immediately became a Cold War icon.

1
ROOTS OF THE COLD WAR

To understand Berlin's unique role in the Cold War is to look back at the turbulent politics of Europe at the turn of the 20th century and trace the different alliances and conflicts as they developed through the First and Second World Wars. These alliances, and in some cases betrayals, helped shape the geopolitical landscape of the first half of the 20th century and turned Berlin into the crucible of the Cold War.

At the start of the 20th century, Europe was in the middle of an unprecedented transformation. Social and political upheaval, massive industrial growth and leaps in military technology threatened the fragile peace. To counter this uncertainty, old alliances between nations were renewed and new alliances brokered to attempt to stave off the threat of invasion by a belligerent enemy.

Some of these affiliations were clearly short term, self-serving and opportunistic, while others were based on shared ideals or mutual trust and were more enduring. By tracing these alliances, it is possible to see how the roots of the Cold War developed and how Berlin found itself on the frontline.

The story begins with the turbulence of the First World War and the twin Russian revolutions of 1917. Three hundred years of Romanov rule was replaced by a Marxist government, headed by Vladimir Illich Ulyanov, much better known by his alias, Lenin, who introduced a new political ideology and dynasty that would become central to the Cold War: Communism. The Triple Entente of Russia, Great Britain and France would eventually prevail over the Central Powers of Germany, Austria-Hungary, Bulgaria and Turkey, but not before Lenin signed a punitive peace treaty with the Germans, handing over swathes of territory, natural resources and cash by way of reparation.[1] It was a terrible start for Lenin's new Bolshevik state, putting it economically years behind the rest of the developed world, however, for Lenin it was a price worth paying in order to get his country out of the imperialist war, and to allow him to concentrate on putting down domestic opposition and completing his revolution. Those brutal territorial concessions would, however, become hot topics for his successors.

What came next would lay the foundations for two further global confrontations that century; the Second World War from 1939 to 1945, immediately followed by the Cold War that lasted until 1991.

The Treaty of Versailles, signed on 28 June 1919, while notionally a peace treaty, would be subsequently blamed for creating the circumstances that brought the world to war again only 20 years later.[2] National humiliation and excessive reparations created the atmosphere in Germany which fuelled a nationalist resurgence, permitting the rise of National Socialism under Adolf Hitler.[3] It also gave Finland, Poland and the Baltic States their independence, prompting further conflict and trading of territory, mostly at the expense of Russia.

Stalin's Grand Plan

With considerable guile, Joseph Vissarionovich Stalin had built up a steely grip on power in the Soviet Union (formed on 30 December 1922), which he was able to cement as Lenin's health failed. Lenin succumbed to a series of strokes on 21 January 1924 and Stalin stepped straight into his big shoes. Over the next decade Stalin established himself as supreme leader of his vast nation, ruthlessly purging all potential opposition.

As a good communist, Stalin had an extensive understanding of history and how it affected the Motherland of Russia (despite being a Georgian). The border between the Soviet Union and the rest of Europe ran from the Baltic Sea in the north to the Black Sea in the south and its length made it particularly vulnerable to invasion, especially across the flat plains of northern Europe. Stalin conceived a masterplan to secure an impenetrable band of territory from the Baltic to the Mediterranean under communist control to act as a buffer zone between the Motherland and its powerful neighbours in Western Europe. In the days before intercontinental ballistic missiles, any Western aggressors would have to cross this territory en route to Russia, and local communist forces, backed by Soviet troops would hopefully stop any advance before it got anywhere near the Soviet Union. Stalin viewed such territory as expendable in defence of the Motherland, especially in the nuclear age that was to come. Equally, the satellite states were there to be 'milked' for resources: food, fuels, raw materials, technology, and knowhow, all heading in one direction – to the east.

Stalin pays a visit to the ailing Lenin at his Dacha, 1922. (Maria Ilyinichna Ulyanova, Public Domain)

Stalin would methodically and ruthlessly impose his ideology throughout his sphere of influence and these 'satellite' or 'client' states would act as a buffer zone on his western flank; a 'Ring of Steel' or 'Iron Curtain'. It was simple, bold, brazen and ruthless and very nearly succeeded.[4] This strategy would remain an obsession for the Soviet leader throughout his life (and for his successors) and proved to be one of the root causes of the Cold War.

Another key factor driving Stalin's strategic world view was communist doctrine, which was at the core of all his decisions. An original Bolshevik and one of Lenin's early acolytes, Stalin was steeped in the works of Karl Marx and Friedrich Engels, the fathers of Marxism, a mindset that was alien to most Westerners. At the heart of his world view was the Communist International (typically abbreviated to Comintern), which was the vehicle to rally (or perhaps control) the progress of the worldwide Communist revolution.[5] Stalin was a fanatic, who truly believed communism was destined to prevail.

Alliances and Betrayals

Despite being at opposite ends of the political spectrum, Hitler and Stalin had one thing in common: the desire to grow their territory, in Hitler's case as 'Lebensraum' or 'living space'. Stalin had eyes on the Baltic States, parts of Finland, Bessarabia (now mostly Moldova and part of north-eastern Ukraine) and Eastern Poland – these had been part of Russia under the Tsars and lost through war (including the Brest-Litovsk and Versailles agreements) but Stalin saw them as legitimate parts of the Soviet Union.

Secret negotiations between the two powers began and on 23 August 1939, the Soviet Union shocked the world by announcing a

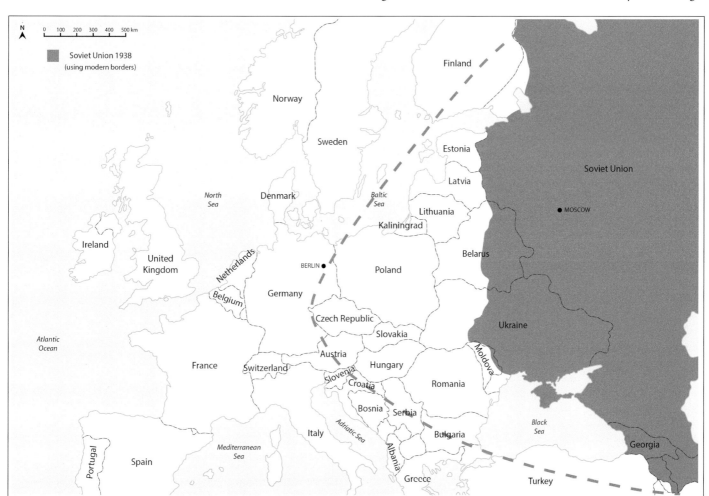

The Soviet Union as it was in 1938. The Treaty of Riga in 1921 gave portions of Belarus and Ukraine to Poland. The dotted line shows the arc of Stalin's 'Ring of Steel', protecting Mother Russia from the Western threat. See map on page 29 to compare the situation in 1948 . (George Anderson)

Soviet Foreign Minister Vyacheslav Molotov signs the German-Soviet Treaty of Friendship in Moscow, 28 September 1939. Behind him are Richard Schulze-Kossens (Ribbentrop's adjutant), Boris Shaposhnikov (Red Army Chief of the General Staff), Joachim von Ribbentrop, Joseph Stalin, Vladimir Pavlov (Soviet translator). Alexey Shkvarzev (Soviet ambassador in Berlin) stands next to Molotov. (US National Archives)

non-aggression pact with the Third Reich. The agreement was signed by Soviet Foreign Minister Vyacheslav Molotov and German Foreign Minister Joachim von Ribbentrop and became known as the Molotov-Ribbentrop Pact.

As well as pledging neutrality in case of war with a third party, there was a secret agreement to carve up Eastern Europe and the Baltic States between German and Soviet interests. Germany would take western Poland, while the Soviets would take Finland and eastern Poland, with the demarcation line to be similar to the Curzon Line, as created by British Foreign Secretary George Curzon after the end of the First World War.

The Molotov-Ribbentrop Pact was a win-win for both parties – Germany gained the freedom to seize half of Poland without provoking a response from Russia, and Stalin would regain his lost territories. Reverberations would be felt throughout the communist world as many 'dyed in the wool' comrades struggled to come to terms with Stalin's apparent sell-out to their natural enemy. Internationally, the world looked on in fear as these two superpowers cosied up together.

On 1 September 1939, the Germans invaded Poland from the south and west, and a few weeks later, on the 17 September 1939, the Soviets invaded eastern Poland as per their agreement with Germany. The campaign was quick, with hostilities ending on 6 October and the country was partitioned along the Curzon Line as per the Molotov-Ribbentrop Pact. Great Britain declared war on Germany on 3 September 1939, having pledged to intervene if Poland's sovereignty was threatened. The Second World War had begun.

Stalin moved quickly with the next phase of his plan, the securing of Leningrad, Russia's second city, by invading and annexing in November 1939 a large part of southern Finland. He then turned to the Baltic States, forcing them to sign 'mutual assistance pacts' and accept Soviet-friendly communist administrations. However, these territorial gains would be short lived as Hitler betrayed the Molotov-Ribbentrop Pact, and on 22 June 1941 invaded the Soviet Union in Operation Barbarossa. Almost all the Soviet gains would be overrun by the Nazi advance.

The Special Relationship

While alliances were being formed, and then betrayed in central Europe, another key relationship was being formed across the Atlantic, which would prove central to the Cold War. Despite Congress' isolationist tendencies, US President Franklin D. Roosevelt (FDR) made a point of reaching out to Great Britain as dark clouds began to gather over Europe. In June 1939, he invited the King and Queen to Washington, the first time a reigning British Monarch had set foot on American soil. He also reached out to Winston Churchill while he was still First Lord of the Admiralty, having sensed that he was going to play a lead role in the forthcoming conflict.

Once war had broken out, Churchill closely courted the American leader, writing to him almost every day in order to secure the materiel needed to fight the war. Great Britain was in desperate straits, with its Expeditionary Force being pushed back towards the sea by Hitler's armies.

Roosevelt was sympathetic to Churchill's plight, but had to tread a very fine line with Congress and the majority of the American people

Royal Navy and US Navy sailors inspect depth charges aboard Wickes-class destroyers, in 1940. In the background are USS *Buchanan* (DD-131), and USS *Crowninshield* (DD-134). On 9 September 1940 both were transferred to the Royal Navy. *Buchanan* became HMS *Campbeltown* (I42), which was expended as a demolition ship during St. Nazaire Raid on 29 March 1942. *Crowninshield* became HMS *Chelsea* (I35) which was transferred to Russia on 16 July 1944 and renamed *Derzkiy*. She was finally returned to the UK for scrapping on 23 June 1949. (US Library of Congress)

Thompson submachine guns, or 'Tommy guns', being uncrated at an ordnance depot in the UK after their arrival from the US through the Lend-Lease scheme, 23 March 1942. (Public Domain)

North American P-51A Mustangs on board ship en route to the UK. In RAF service they were known as Mustang Ia or Mustang II. (US National Archives)

remaining isolationist. The US President, however, recognised that giving Hitler free rein over Europe would not be in the best long-term interests of the United States. FDR decided that the United States *should* help the British out in their hour of need, and the extraordinary success of the Battle of Britain and the 'miracle' of Dunkirk appeared to vindicate his judgement.

Although it would not be called this until 1946, the US-UK 'Special Relationship' began on 2 September 1940 when Roosevelt signed the famous 'Destroyers for Bases' agreement.[6] Great Britain was in desperate need for ships to protect the convoy routes, bringing essential supplies from all over the world. The US needed a network of bases at strategic locations around the world as it began to project itself as more of a global player, which the British possessed in abundance. The deal was simple: Roosevelt offered around 50 First World War-vintage destroyers in exchange for air and sea bases in Newfoundland and across the Caribbean: a great deal for the Americans, but a lifeline for the British.

1941 would prove to be a critical year for relationships on both sides of the Atlantic. The next chapter in this 'Special Relationship' came on 11 March 1941 when the US Lend-Lease Act came into force.[7] Despite remaining neutral and publicly isolationist, Roosevelt introduced this bill 'To sell, transfer title to, exchange, lease, lend, or otherwise dispose of military equipment of all types to foreign powers with the ultimate objective of the defense of the United States.' Payment was not expected immediately, in effect 'lending' the materiel to the Foreign Power. 'Foreign Powers' at this stage meant Great Britain, although aid also eventually flowed to the Republic of China, the Soviet Union, Free France and more than 30 countries, dispensing some $50 billion (at 1940s prices) worth of material in assistance. After months of negotiation, the 'consideration' offered by the British government in return for much of the aid was 'joint action directed towards the creation of a liberalized [*sic*] international economic order in the post-war world,' that is, taking the fight to the Nazis.

It also helped to temporarily deflect the growing international pressure on Roosevelt to join the fight. While much of the materiel supplied during the actual war was provided free, the US also provided huge loans and lines of credit that would help an almost bankrupt Britain recover after the war. The UK only made its final repayment to the US in 2006.

Allies

While the relationship between Great Britain and the United States was getting stronger and stronger, the situation in Europe changed dramatically on 22 June 1941 when Hitler reneged on his non-aggression pact and invaded the Soviet Union. Hitler was now fighting on two fronts, and Stalin was looking for new allies.

Great Britain and the Soviet Union (with the United States still waiting in the wings) were not particularly natural bedfellows. The US and UK shared a language and a common culture but still had their differences, however, the Soviet Union was a different beast altogether. The communist state and Stalin's totalitarian dictatorship were probably as much of a natural enemy to the Anglo-American partnership as the Germans, and Churchill remained acutely suspicious of Stalin's motivations throughout the war.

However, Churchill, knowing a partnership between the Soviet Union and Great Britain would hasten the fall of the Third Reich, reached out to the Soviet leader, offering all possible military aid. Britain's 'pact with the devil' was signed in Moscow on 12 July 1941 and was short and to the point:

1 The two Governments mutually undertake to render each other assistance and support of all kinds in the present war against Hitlerite Germany.

2 They further undertake that during this war they will neither negotiate nor conclude an armistice or treaty of peace except by mutual agreement.[8]

Winston Churchill and Franklin D. Roosevelt on board USS *Augusta* for the Atlantic Conference 9 August 1941. (US Navy)

included huge numbers of trucks, jeeps, aircraft, guns and other much needed supplies that gave Stalin (and Churchill) a huge boost at a critical moment in the war. Combined with the Anglo-American 'Destroyers for Bases' programme, this represented an unprecedented and extremely generous gesture of international support from an otherwise neutral power.

Everything changed yet again on 7 December 1941 when the Empire of Japan unleashed a surprise aerial attack on the US fleet moored at Pearl Harbor in Hawaii, bringing America into the war.[11] Churchill got his wish, and the immense economic power of the United States joined the British Empire in the second World War of the 20th century.

The first face to face meeting between Churchill and Roosevelt took place in Washington from 22 December 1941 to 14 January 1942 (codenamed Arcadia).

The first convoy left Scapa Flow heading for Murmansk the following month. On the face of it, the British were providing moral and materiel support to Stalin, but it was more about getting Stalin on Churchill's side, stopping him negotiating a separate peace (or another alliance) with Germany, and distracting Hitler while the British regrouped in the west. The British Prime Minister knew, however, that the agreement was not worth the paper it was written on and remained acutely suspicious of his new ally, but for the time being, it was an alliance worth having.

In the meantime, Churchill met Roosevelt in Newfoundland, where they discussed how the war was going for Great Britain, the Soviet Union's entry into the conflict and developed a common position on matters of mutual interest. The Placentia Bay Conference (also known as the Atlantic Conference, codename Riviera) was held from 9 to 11 August 1941, cemented the 'Special Relationship' between the two leaders and was to have a major influence on geo-politics for decades to come.[9]

The resulting 'Atlantic Charter' set out a vision of a post-war 'new world order' and a common set of values, which would prove to be the genesis of the United Nations (UN) and NATO. The statement included a declaration that neither the UK or US wished to grow their respective territories through hostile action (unlike Hitler's 'Lebensraum' and Stalin's overtures on Eastern Europe) and statements of the basic tenets of democratic government: self-determination, free trade, economic and social advancement, assured collective security and a commitment to disarmament.[10]

The three Allied nations came together for the first time at the first Moscow Conference (codenamed Caviar), which took place between 29 September and 1 October 1941. The US envoy reassured Stalin that although they were remaining neutral in the fight against the Nazis, they would support him with materiel and agreed terms to begin Lend-Lease shipments via the treacherous Arctic convoys. These shipments

They confirmed that Germany would be their initial focus before moving on to tackle the Japanese, and developed ideas from the Atlantic Conference into 'The Declaration by The United Nations'.[12] This important document was published on 1 January 1942 and pledged the 26 signatory governments to the maximum war effort against the Berlin-Rome-Tokyo Axis and bound them against making a separate peace. Crucially, it tied the fate of the USSR in with that of the US and United Kingdom, as well as further cementing the alliance that would go on to form the UN and NATO.

The relationship between the three Allies would prove to be the deciding factor for the success of the Allied campaign, although it required a lot of patience, determination and compromise from all sides. The leaders and their senior representatives would go on to meet regularly as the war progressed.[13] There was a fascinating dynamic developing between the three nations. Despite being allies, they never fully trusted each other. Churchill met Roosevelt face to face on numerous occasions and he would also meet Stalin one on one, but Churchill would never let Roosevelt meet Stalin without him being present, which irritated Roosevelt immensely. Churchill was acutely aware of the fragility of his position at the 'top table' and feared being side-lined in a bilateral US-USSR deal. Roosevelt also feared that Churchill would unilaterally negotiate a side deal with Stalin, which was a very reasonable concern, given the British stateman's past form on that front.[14] Stalin did not trust anyone but was prepared to play the British and the Americans off against each other for his own benefit. It would not be until November 1943 before the Big Three leaders would meet for the first time in Tehran.

A further summit meeting took place in Moscow from 19 October to 30 October 1943. Looking to a future peace, the Allies decided to establish a European Advisory Commission (EAC) composed of representatives of the three powers.[15] The Commission was to be based in London with the presidency rotating between the three members.

The Commission was tasked with sketching out the end of the war: the detailed terms of unconditional surrender for the Germans; the post-war map of Europe; and proposing how it would be administered under occupation, including the delightfully termed 'Dismemberment of Germany.' The EAC was set to begin its work in the new year, but before then, the leaders of the Big Three Allied powers would finally meet face to face.

The Big Three

Two years and five months after the Soviets joined the war on the side of the Allies and 23 months after Pearl Harbor, Roosevelt, Churchill and Stalin finally met in Tehran, the first of only three Big Three summit meetings of the war. They agreed a grand strategy on how to defeat the Axis and argued about how the world should look once the Axis was defeated. Under the pretence of inter-Allied cordiality, these three conferences would play host to high drama, bringing out the very best and the very worst in the wartime alliances and decisions made and more importantly decisions omitted, would have serious implications for the next five decades.

The Tehran Conference (codenamed Eureka) was held primarily in the Soviet Embassy in Tehran, Iran from 28 November to 1 December 1943. Iran, with its rich oil fields, was of strategic interest to all parties in the war, and the choice of venue was highly significant. On one hand, it signified to the world that the Allies were committed to maintaining Iran's independence, but also that none of the attendees would be allowed to get away with claiming the oil fields as theirs. Allies were allies but were still independent nations and both Stalin and Churchill had form when it came to territorial raiding.

The most important outcome of the conference was the decision on the much awaited 'Second Front', what became known as Operation Overlord. Roosevelt and Stalin ganged up on Churchill to target the planned D-Day landings for May or June 1944 on the north coast of France, as opposed to Churchill's preferred second front from the Mediterranean. Stalin agreed to launch another offensive on the Eastern Front to divide Hitler's attention and also agreed to take up the fight with Japan after the defeat of Germany.

Although acquired under the fateful Molotov-Ribbentrop Pact, Stalin was particularly keen to legitimise the territorial gains he had made in Poland and the Baltic States with his new allies, and naively, they went along with him.

The EAC began work in London on 14 January 1944 with the war going in their favour, and by September, they had come up with a proposal to divide up Germany within the frontiers she had on the 31 December 1937, before Hitler really began his expansionist efforts. It proposed the division of post-war Germany into three Zones of Occupation, each controlled by one of the Big Three. Berlin would also be split three ways, with the Soviet Union quick to claim the eastern part of Germany and the north-eastern sector of Berlin as theirs, while the US and UK Zones were left vague at this stage. The French were not included in the discussions.

By the end of the year, the British and Americans were allocated zones of Germany which roughly reflected the direction their respective advances took. The British were given the north-western part of Germany and the US the south-western corner. The proposed split of Berlin was along similar lines, but this would not be formalised until Potsdam. On 11 November 1944, the existing members of the EAC invited France to join the Commission and at Yalta in February 1945, the leaders agreed to give the French a slice of the pie. The Soviets were not prepared to give up any of their territory and generally had little time for France's demands – the Soviets lost millions of lives in the conflict and felt their suffering considerably outweighed that of the French. The French had also played a much smaller role in the advance on Germany. As it was the British and Americans who were pushing for France's inclusion at the post-war top table, the French sector had to come out of their territory. The British were more than happy to relinquish some and allocated a triangle of their zone in the south-west of Germany to their French allies. The territory bordered France anyway, and would reduce the cost of policing and administering the Zone of Occupation to the nearly bankrupt British post-war exchequer. The Americans did likewise.

Towards the end of 1944, the EAC also came up with the idea of the tri-partite Allied Control Council (ACC, *Alliierter Kontrollrat* in German), which would ensure the unconditional surrender went ahead smoothly, and would be tasked with governing Germany after the surrender.

As an additional point, they proposed a similar partition for Austria and Vienna, to formally separate Austria from Germany and establish its own democratically elected government. They also reached out to all the other European states, many of whom had been occupied by the Nazis, ensuring that the terms of Germany's surrender were being applied universally.

Stalin, Roosevelt and Churchill at the Tehran Conference, November 1943. (US Navy)

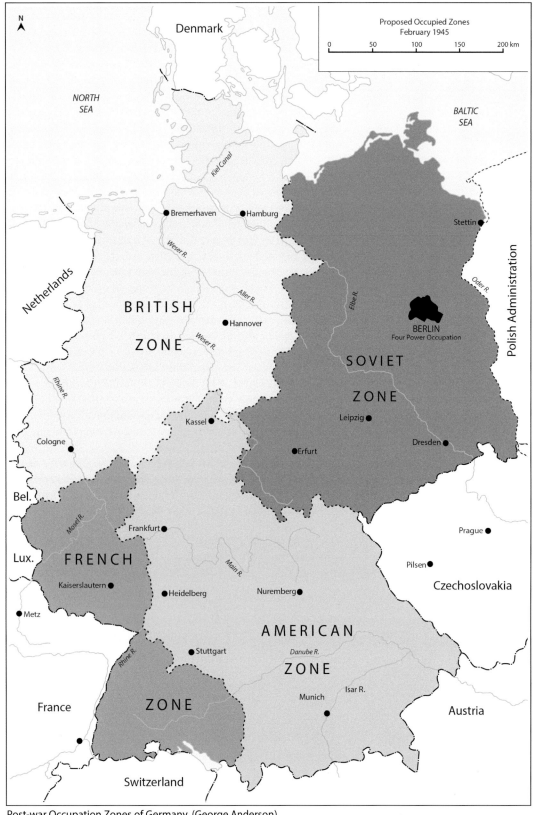

Post-war Occupation Zones of Germany. (George Anderson)

With the invasion of Europe well underway from the west and the Red Army pressurising the Nazis on a second front in the east, the leaders came together again from the 4 to 11 February 1945 in the Crimean coastal resort of Yalta for the second Big Three meeting to plan the end of the Third Reich and agree on the post-war map of Europe. This conference (also known as the Crimea Conference and codenamed Argonaut or Magneto, depending on which side of the Atlantic you were from) was to have a major impact on the future of Berlin and the Cold War.

They all agreed that the ultimate fate of Germany was key to the peace and stability of post-war Europe, but each of the Allies had a different view of what a post-war Germany should look like. However, they agreed that Germany's surrender would have to be unconditional and the country would be split between the four Allied powers; Great Britain, the United States, the Soviet Union and France as per the EAC's recommendations, although Stalin hoped he could eventually include a unified Communist Germany behind his defensive 'Iron Curtain'. He also intended to enthusiastically play the part of conqueror and methodically pick his zone clean of resources by way of reparations. The French, on the other hand, having been at the sharp end of German aggression twice in the previous half century wanted to keep Germany divided and emasculated. Great Britain and America shared Stalin's hopes for a unified Germany, but under very different conditions – as a democratic independent federalised state.

When carefully drafting the surrender terms for Germany's capitulation throughout 1944, the EAC overlooked the fact that the German government, who would be required to sign any official surrender document, might have ceased to exist by the time victory was won, especially as the Allies advanced on Berlin. With no meaningful government to negotiate with, how would the Allies facilitate the transition from military rule (martial law) to some semblance of civilian rule, albeit under the auspices of the occupying powers?

They did, however, agree how Germany would be demilitarised (including the de-Nazification processes), but they argued about the way war reparations would be paid – the row would endure through to Potsdam and beyond. The Soviets had demanded a heavy price from Germany, pushing for half of all the reparations due, while the US countered with a proposal that each of the Allies could only 'extract' reparations from their *own* Zone of Occupation. Roosevelt agreed on an arbitrary figure of $20 billion (with Stalin expecting $10 billion

British Prime Minister Winston Churchill, US President Franklin Roosevelt, and Soviet leader Joseph Stalin met at Yalta in February 1945 to discuss their joint occupation of Germany and plans for post-war Europe. Behind them stand, from the left, Field Marshal Sir Alan Brooke, Fleet Admiral Ernest King, Fleet Admiral William D. Leahy, General of the Army George Marshall, Major General Laurence S. Kuter, General Aleksei Antonov, Vice Admiral Stepan Kucherov, and Admiral of the Fleet Nikolay Kuznetsov. February 1945. (US National Archives)

Surrender of Germany, 7 May 1945. View in SHAEF Forward HQ., at Reims, France, following signing of the German "Unconditional Surrender". Left to right: General of the Artillery of the Red Army Ivan Alexeyevich Susloparov; Lieutenant General Sir Frederick E. Morgan, Deputy Chief of Staff, SHAEF; Lieutenant General Walter Bedell Smith, Chief of Staff, SHAEF; Captain Harry D. Butcher, SHAEF Naval Aide; General Dwight D. Eisenhower, Supreme Allied Commander, holding pens with which the surrender was signed; Air Chief Marshal Sir Arthur Tedder, Deputy Supreme Commander; and Admiral Sir Harold M. Burrough, Allied Naval Chief. (US National Archives)

of that), a compromise that he hoped would avoid a repeat of the German people's total humiliation after Versailles, which many blamed for the rise of Nazism.[16]

Stalin did agree to open up another front in the Far East once the Nazis were beaten and direct his considerable military might against the Japanese. He promised to do this within three months of the German capitulation. Stalin also got his allies to agree to his proposal for the Soviet Union's western border with Poland, that is, the Curzon Line. He quickly installed a pro-Soviet government in Warsaw, thus ensuring Poland formed a key part of his buffer zone with the West.

With Stalin regrouping at the Oder, General Eisenhower – the Supreme Commander of British and American forces – also stopped his eastward advance on 12 April 1945 at the River Elbe, near Magdeburg, some 50 miles from Berlin. Conventional wisdom has this decision to stop short of Berlin as a political concession made by Roosevelt at the Yalta Conference, giving Stalin the 'prize' of Berlin, although post-war analysis has revealed that it was more down to military expediency, pragmatism, and the intention to minimise 'blue on blue' ('friendly fire') incidents and US casualties.[17]

However, back in the USA, the death of US President Franklin D. Roosevelt would cause shockwaves through the Allied coalition. Roosevelt's health had been declining for some time, and both his November 1944 General Election win and the Yalta Conference in February 1945 had put him under intense pressure. He succumbed to a stroke on 14 April 1945 while at Warm Springs, Georgia, his favourite retreat, and was succeeded by his Vice President of 82 days, Harry S. Truman, that same day.[18]

Truman had little foreign policy experience and lacked

FDR's international gravitas but was sure of America's place in the world and convinced that he could handle Stalin. This was not to be the case, and the relationship between the Soviet Union and the USA deteriorated rapidly thereafter, with Truman's administration clashing over the Soviet influence on Eastern Europe and the future role of the UN. In addition, his relationship with Churchill lacked the depth of trust and warmth that Churchill enjoyed with Roosevelt and this would weaken the Allied position at Potsdam. As the war drew to a close, the warm feelings of cooperation and common purpose evaporated and as the leaders reconvened in Potsdam, hostility and suspicion replaced the positivity seen at the previous meetings.

Students of Stalin's track record in manipulating partners (such as the Molotov-Ribbentrop non-aggression pact of August 1939) would not have been surprised to see Stalin 'drop' his former allies when they had ceased to be of use to him. Whether Churchill and Roosevelt were 'played' by the Soviet leader or whether they knowingly went along with him, knowing that winning the war against Hitler (and also possibly Japan) was dependent on Soviet involvement, remains one of the unanswered questions of the Second World War. However, Roosevelt was subsequently criticised for 'handing over' Eastern Europe and north-east Asia to communism and laying the foundations for the Cold War.

The Red Army began their assault on the heart of the Third Reich on 16 April, backed by over a million troops and over 20,000 tanks and artillery pieces, beginning a bloody and brutal attack on the city.

The ever-prescient Winston Churchill wrote to Stalin on 28 April 1945, providing us with a fairly accurate description of what would soon become the Cold War:

> We cannot be happy looking at a future where you and the countries you dominate, together with the Communist parties in many other countries, would be on one side and the nations allied to the English-speaking countries and their dominions be on the other! Such confrontation would lead the world to ruin, and those among us from whichever side who had any responsibility would bear the shame of when the history of that period came to be written.[19]

On 30 April 1945, after two weeks of absolute carnage, and with the Red Army only a few hundred metres from his bunker in central Berlin, Adolf Hitler committed suicide. The Nazi infrastructure collapsed within days and on 7 May, at SHAEF (Supreme Headquarters Allied Expeditionary Force) in Reims, north-eastern France, General Alfred Jodl, signed the unconditional surrender of all German forces. Stalin demanded his own surrender ceremony, so on the following day, 8 May, the Germans were forced to 'surrender' for a second time. 8 May was declared a public holiday in Great Britain as 'Victory in Europe Day' (VE Day) and continues to be celebrated to this day.

2

BERLIN: FRONTLINE CITY

Once the Nazis had surrendered, the need for a firm legal basis to govern post-war Germany became critical, so on the 9 May 1945, the day after the surrender, the EAC were somewhat belatedly given the task of rapidly resolving the matter. By the end of the month, they produced the 'Declaration regarding the defeat of Germany and the assumption of supreme authority by the Allied powers,' which converted the previous *surrender* document into a declaration of *authority*, with supreme power vested in the commanders in chief of the armed forces of the three Allied powers in each of their Zones of Occupation, to be administered via the ACC (the French were included later).[1] The 'Berlin Declaration' was signed by General Eisenhower, Field Marshall Montgomery and Marshall Zhukov on 5 June 1945, with the ACC immediately assuming authority over central and local government across the country and all remaining armed forces. The surviving troops were immediately ordered to disarm and surrender as POWs and the Allies took control of

all remaining military assets: aircraft; ships; armaments; installations; and infrastructure. All Allied POWs were to be immediately released. Only the civil police would be allowed to keep their small arms for the purpose of maintaining law and order. Further to the work of the EAC

The Brandenburg Gate in Berlin in July 1945. (Truman Library)

The Soviet Zone of eastern Germany and position of Berlin. (George Anderson)

fight, but he may be able to start by squeezing them out of Berlin, giving him free rein over all of eastern Germany.

Germany's capital city, Berlin, was located deep in the Soviet Zone of Germany but the other Allies were not willing to leave Hitler's symbolic capital exclusively to the Soviets. To the conquering armies, Berlin was symbolic of their very costly victory over the Nazis and the rubble strewn streets and avenues of the city represented far more than just a point on the map. All of the Allies knew Berlin would become a vitally important part of the new European order.

Because of this special attachment, an uncomfortable four-way power-sharing compromise had been agreed between the four former allies via the work of the EAC, a decision that would condemn the city to be a geopolitical tinderbox for decades to come. The city was divided into four sectors reflecting the split of the rest of Germany. The British, American and French sectors became a Western capitalist 'island' in a 'sea' of communism. They would become surrounded and vastly outnumbered by Soviet troops.

Before the war, Berlin was a thriving metropolis, the centre of German political and cultural life. The population in 1939 was around 4.3 million, which had fallen to around 3.3 million in 1945, with as many as 50,000 people killed in bombing raids, with many thousands still buried under the rubble of what remained of the city. The smell of death and decay hovered over the ruins of the German capital.

and the various wartime conferences, the ACC was now in charge of Germany. That was the theory, at least …

The occupation zone allocated to Stalin reached up to the Mecklenburg region of the Baltic coast, which included the key port city of Rostock and down to the border with Czechoslovakia, which was well on the way to becoming a Soviet Satellite. If he could gain control of western Germany, the sectors currently occupied by the Americans, British and French, then his buffer would extend all the way down to Switzerland, Austria and the protective band of the Alps. His erstwhile allies were unlikely to hand over their sectors without a

By spring 1945, Berlin was a shattered city, pounded by Allied bombing and blasted by advancing Soviet troops as the Third Reich crumbled around them. The destruction was on an epic scale with around 40 percent of the city's buildings flattened. The landscape was post-apocalyptic, albeit not as bad as fire-stormed Dresden or the atomic devastation that was to come at Hiroshima and Nagasaki. Wrecked vehicles and trams littered the streets and power, water and sewage utilities had long since packed up. A quarter of the subway system was flooded and of the 225 bridges in the city, 140 were destroyed, blocking waterways that had been vital to the city's

Scene of destruction in Berlin, Germany, 1945. (Edwin Pauley via Truman Library)

Spree River Bridge amongst ruins of Berlin. (Truman Library)

Damaged buildings, Berlin, July 1946. (Jones J. Weldon via Truman Library)

Scene of destruction, Berlin, July 1946. (Edwin W. Pauley via Truman library)

transport infrastructure. That said, there were patches of the city that survived relatively unscathed, for example, the district of Prenzlauer Berg north-east of Alexanderplatz lost only 20 percent of its buildings, while over in the west of the city, the Mitte district lost two thirds. The Soviet sector was hit particularly hard, a result of the Red Army's brutal advance.[2]

War is brutal for all concerned, but especially for innocent civilians, who happen to get caught up in the fighting. The advancing Red Army, however, took this brutality to levels more associated with ancient or medieval history. The Red Army was highly politicised, with Commissars and a very efficient propaganda machine bombarding the rank-and-file with Marxist theory and tales of the horrors of Nazi occupation. As the troops marched on Germany, they were flooded with bloodthirsty messages of revenge and retribution due to all Germans, not just those in uniform. Newspapers were full of articles reminding the reader of Nazi atrocities, stirring lectures were sat through, pamphlets were handed out in mess tents and roadside

banners implored the advancing troops to reap unrelenting violence on Germany, and all it stood for.

The vanguards of General Zhukov and Konev's armies were for the most part professional, battle hardened troops, but as soon as victory was won and their common purpose had gone, the thin veneer of discipline disappeared and the Red Army began a rampage of murder, rape and looting, weaponising violent (and mostly sexual) assault as a tool of vengeance, exacerbated with the arrival of lower quality rear-echelon troops. The Soviet officer corps, so depleted by Stalin's purges, struggled to keep discipline at the best of times, but found it almost impossible to stop the violence against the German civilian population, especially as many approved of it. It soon became clear that the army could not adapt to become a successful peacetime government and so in June 1945, it was relieved of its governing duties to be replaced by the Soviet Military Administration in Germany, known variously as SMA, SMAG (*Sovyetskaya Voyennaya Administratsiya v Germanii*), SVAG or SMAD (*Sowjetische Militäradministration in Deutschland*). The SMA inherited an almost impossible situation, being vastly outnumbered by Red Army troops who did not report to them, with a demotivated and complicit officer corps and with conflicting loyalties in Moscow. SMA staff would arrest known offenders, only to have their armed comrades (and often their officers) break them out of

An armed Soviet soldier leans against a pillar and watches citizens walking on a street in Berlin, Germany. In the background are buildings damaged by bombing in the Second World War. (Barney Ricketts via Truman Library)

Walter Ulbricht in 1949. (Deutsche Fotothek)

jail.[3] The conflict between the two erupted into fist fights and even gun fights around barracks, bars, cinemas and in the streets.

Active and demobbed Red Army troops also carried their wartime violence into the post-war peace in most of the other Soviet occupied territories, but new Soviet puppet governments were soon installed, and the violence was quickly brought under control. In Germany, however, the unusual power-sharing arrangement and sheer number of troops created a situation where violence flourished. The SMA did not really get a grip on things until 1947.

Berlin's hospitals estimated the number of rape victims in Berlin to be between 95,000 and 130,000 women, and around ten percent of them would subsequently die, mostly from suicide.[4] The number of rapes and the death rate was much higher throughout the rest of the Soviet Zone, with as many as two million German women being raped as the Red Army advanced, many being violated multiple times. Thousands of unwanted pregnancies and sexually transmitted diseases would result. War is always traumatising for civilians, but this wave of wholesale, unchecked and partly state-sponsored sexual violence would deeply traumatise a whole generation in the eastern occupation zone – a troubling start to what would become the DDR.

Enter the Communists

If the first part of Stalin's grand plan for Europe involved wholesale land grabbing, the second part involved imposing communism all across this territory. As history shows us, he had a tried-and-tested model that he applied time and time again.[5]

Communism had been a feature of German politics since the end of the 19th century – Karl Marx and Friedrich Engels were Germans after all, and the German Communist Party (the *Kommunistische Partei Deutschlands* or KPD) was formed on 30 December 1918 by the Spartacus League, headed by Rosa Luxemburg and Karl Liebknecht.[6]

A young Walter Ulbricht rose through the ranks, receiving ideological training in Moscow and becoming involved in the Comintern, Stalin's vehicle for spreading communism internationally and maintaining an iron grip on its disciples around the world.[7] Ulbricht became a member of the German Reichstag and was elected as KPD leader for Berlin and the State of Brandenburg. With the Nazis in power, Ulbricht and fellow Communist veteran, Wilhelm Pieck managed to escape to Moscow, where they continued to represent the KPD and Comintern in exile while the Second World War raged across the globe.[8] A Young Communist organiser called Erich Honecker was less fortunate, being arrested by the Gestapo and imprisoned in Brandenburg Prison.[9] When the Red Army took Berlin in 1945, he was quickly released because of his impeccable communist credentials.

Stalin's proven technique was to use local communists to agitate and infiltrate local politics, building a position from where they could quietly take over. On the eve of victory, a group of ten German communists led by Ulbricht (which became known as the Ulbricht Group) was flown in to join Marshall Zhukov's army just outside of Berlin. A second group of ten, under Anton Ackermann, was sent to join Marshall Konev's troops, then approaching Dresden. A final group under Gustav Sobottka were sent to join the advance at Mecklenburg in the north. These were all committed German communists who had spent most of the last decade in exile under the care of the Soviet Union. Their task was to set up local German government (albeit with a communist slant) as soon as the fighting had stopped and before any other influences (that is, the other Allies) arrived.

Ulbricht's group arrived in the city on 2 May 1945, the day the city capitulated but a week before the overall German surrender. Each member was given a section of the city and with the backing of Soviet commanders, began organising the local neighbourhoods. At this stage, there was no oversight or presence of the other Allies, so the Soviets and Ulbricht's men were left to work unhindered.

The 'Regime of Deputies' was a key political strategy for the Soviets: establish 'acceptable' and 'respectable' figureheads in key positions throughout the new German administration, while ensuring the real power lay with their communist deputies, who were all hand-picked by Ulbricht on behalf of his Soviet masters. This policy made a show of an inclusive democracy, while all the time it was the Soviets who were calling all the shots. As Walter Ulbricht famously told the members of his group: 'It must appear democratic, but we must control everything.'[10]

These groups of German communist agitators immediately got to work re-establishing local government in the city. Following the principles of the 'Regime of Deputies', they installed local dignitaries as district mayors irrespective of their particular political persuasion,

Wilhelm Pieck, who would become the first (and only) President of the DDR. (Deutsche Fotothek)

just as long as they were avowed anti-fascists. However, if the mayor was not communist, the new deputy mayor certainly was.

On 12 May 1945, Ulbricht arranged for the elderly Dr Arthur Werner to be installed as Lord Mayor for Berlin but also placed a staunch communist, Karl Maron, as Werner's deputy to ensure the Lord Mayor could be easily manipulated – yet another example of the 'Regime of Deputies'. Communists were also similarly installed in all key administrative roles across the city; education, housing, transport, utilities and at police headquarters. A week later, on 19 May 1945, the Berlin city government was re-instituted to take control of public services and local government.

All this political manoeuvring was done quickly to ensure the communists had *their* people in place *before* the other 'Allies' arrived. Once someone was in place, they were harder to unseat, and with so much else to do in the city, the Allies could be temporarily fooled into being satisfied that at least someone was filling the position.

In early June, Pieck arrived in Berlin from Moscow with instructions to restart political activity in the city and across the Soviet Zone – the British, Americans and French still banned any political activity in their Zones of Occupation – and they managed to re-form the KPD by the 10 June 1945. The older Pieck was to be the figurehead of the movement, while Ulbricht manoeuvred in the background as his deputy to ensure that Moscow's wishes were followed.

There should be no doubt that Ulbricht was a total Soviet 'puppet', with a variety of different masters pulling his strings: the Soviet Military Administration in Germany under Marshall Georgi K. Zhukov; the Soviet Military Governor of Germany; the Main Political Administration of the Red Army (PUR) under General Galadshev; and Berlin city commander, Colonel General Bezarin.[11] [12] [13] As was often the case in Soviet Russia, the real power in Berlin lay with Galadshev's deputy, the NKGB's General Ivan Serov.[14] Ulbricht quickly became the public face of the Soviet occupiers.

The Red Army chose the borough of Karlshorst, to the east of Berlin, as their base of operations.[15] They announced on 3 May 1945 that the local population had to vacate their homes to make way for the Soviet military and its administration, giving some 8,000 residents only 24 hours' notice to leave. The SMA shared the site with the NKGB (the predecessor to the KGB), and the site became the Soviet's largest intelligence operation outside Russia.

As soon as the Soviets arrived, their first task was to find and dismantle as much of the surviving German industry as they could and return it to Russia by way of reparations. Under the watchful eye of General Serov and his NKGB troops, the Soviet Zone and much of Berlin was systematically looted, pillaged and left bare, with machinery, equipment, records, wealth, valuables and occasionally people, packaged up and sent east to Russia. They concentrated initially on the areas which were soon to be handed over to the British, Americans and French, and without anybody there to complain, they had a completely free rein to loot what they wanted.

Hearts and Minds

One thing that is particularly notable is the speed by which the Soviets threw their net over the city of Berlin and the rest of the Soviet Zone. While the British and American forces waited west of the Elbe, the Soviets successfully deployed teams to saturate local government with hand-picked communist leaning officials. They then began an all-out 'hearts and minds' campaign aimed at the German population in their zone, trying to create the illusion that some degree of normality had been restored thanks to the efforts of their Soviet 'liberators'. It began immediately after the Nazis capitulated. The administration quickly began securing food supplies to feed the civilians and cracked down on black marketeers. Speculators were rounded up and arrested, and some semblance of law and order was imposed. Almost all the wood (trees, doors, furniture

Emergency food distribution, July 1945. (US Army Military History Institute)

German police round up black marketeers in front of the Reichstag building. (US Army Military History Institute)

etc) had already been stripped for use as firewood, and the Berliners used every patch of free land to try to grow food.

They also began mobilising the citizens of the city to try to tidy the place up. Groups of mostly civilian women were formed into working parties to clear rubble and get services running again. The workers were known as *Trümmerfrauen* – 'women of the rubble'. Whether the women participated out of civic pride or just as forced labour is open to debate, but the main roads, key landmarks and public spaces were soon cleared of the detritus of war.

However, they also attempted to restart Berlin's famed cultural life, an extraordinary feat out of the chaos of war. On 13 May 1945, only 13 days since Hitler had shot himself and five days after the German surrender, the SMA began broadcasting to the citizens of Berlin. The new German language radio service was called *Berliner Rundfunk* and was supervised by Walter Ulbricht. There was, of course, an agenda to this, enabling the mass distribution of Soviet propaganda, but at least it was something. The SMA even succeeded in getting some of Berlin's famous museums re-opened and concerts restarted, albeit in temporary locations.

On 19 May, the first post-war newspaper was published, albeit as a Soviet propaganda sheet. By starting up their own printing presses, or taking over existing newspapers, they would control the narrative and thus, indirectly control the population – a tried-and-tested technique dating back to before the Russian Revolution. Having total control over the media back in the Soviet Union, it was relatively straightforward to apply the same techniques and exploit the shattered post-war German society, which welcomed *any* news, whether or not it was independent. There had not been a 'free' press in Germany since before the rise of the Nazis and anything that was not out of Joseph Goebbels Propaganda ministry was welcome.

The first proper newspapers that appeared in the Soviet Zone were produced by the new post-war political parties and as the parties were heavily influenced by the Soviet Military Administration, the content followed a distinctly Soviet agenda. The *Deutsche Volkszeitung* (or DVZ) was the mouthpiece of the KPD, while *Das Volk* spoke for the SPD. It is worth remembering that all this had happened *before* the British, American and French forces had been allowed into the city.

Book publishing was also restarted but under strict supervision to ensure that *all* reading matter followed the party line. *Verlag Neuer Weg* was set up as the official publishing house of the German Communist Party on 30 July 1945, while *Kulturbund zur Demokratischen Erneuerung Deutschlands* (Democratic Cultural Alliance for the Renewal of Germany) received its licence on 18 August 1945. The launch of *Verlag Volk und Wissen* (People and Knowledge Publishing House) at the same time tapped into the huge demand for schoolbooks after the war and they went on to publish some 55 million textbooks

Soviet traffic control, Berlin. (Edwin W, Pauley via Truman Library)

Allotment gardens to the right of the ruins of the Reichstag. (Edwin W, Pauley via Truman Library)

The *Trümmerfrauen* – Berlin women cleaning and sorting bricks from bomb sites. (Deutsche Fotothek)

over the next four years, all with content approved by the East German (and therefore Soviet) authorities.

These proactive and generally positive initiatives are in sharp contrast to the quasi officially sanctioned wave of brutal sexual assaults that accompanied the Red Army's advance and early days of occupation. It is perplexing to view both these 'campaigns' side by side – oppression via mass rape vs. a cultural reawakening for the German people. Arguably, Stalin had an external audience in mind for the 'hearts and minds' campaign, demonstrating to the world how the Soviet system could conquer both militarily and culturally. Certainly, the true scale of the sexual assaults still remained a taboo subject long after the formation of the DDR, while the cultural initiatives received lavish publicity.

The Soviets also moved quickly to commemorate their war dead, in particular, the estimated 80,000 Red Army troops who died taking Berlin. The first monument included two Soviet T-34 tanks, that were allegedly the first to reach Berlin, and two artillery pieces. The large Russian inscription is translated as "Eternal glory to heroes who fell in battle with the German fascist invaders for the freedom and independence of the Soviet Union. 1941–1945." The memorial is located in Tiergarten, just down from the Brandenburg Gate. Perplexingly, it is within the British sector, which would prove problematic after the Berlin Wall went up. It seems clear that at that stage, the

Soviets did not expect their Western neighbours to remain in the city for long.

Further memorials were built in Treptow Park and Schönholzer Heide, both completed in 1949 and located in the Soviet sector.

Meanwhile, across the Atlantic in San Francisco, representatives of 46 countries (which would eventually increase to 50) had been meeting to continue the work began at the Atlantic Conference back in 1941, which would result in the United Nations Charter.[16] It was signed at a ceremony at the Veterans' Memorial Hall in San Francisco

The San Francisco Conference, 25 April – 26 June 1945: United Kingdom signs the United Nations Charter. The Earl of Halifax, Ambassador to the United States; member of the Delegation from the United Kingdom, signing the United Nations Charter at a ceremony held at the Veterans' War Memorial Building, San Francisco, United States, 26 June 1945. (UN Multimedia)

Soviet Great Patriotic War Memorial, Tiergarten, Berlin, 1945. (Donald S. Dawson via Truman Library)

Office of Military Government of the US (OMGUS) Offices, Berlin, July 1946. (Edwin W, Pauley via Truman Library)

US GIs relax against an M8 Greyhound armoured car, armed with an M2 Browning .50 calibre heavy machine gun, with bombed out buildings and German civilians in the background. (Albert Grandolini)

had acted on their promises. However, Truman did not want to upset the Soviets and overruled Churchill, so the Western Allies withdrew only to be replaced by Soviet forces who raped and imposed their will over this new territory, just as they had further east and in Berlin.

The first US attempt to enter Berlin took place on 23 June 1945, when a Preliminary Reconnaissance Party headed off from the US Zone towards the city. They got as far as Babelsberg, then still a distinct town to the south-west of Berlin, before being stopped by Soviet officers, objecting to the number of vehicles in the reconnaissance party. The Soviets stood their ground and the Americans had to turn back, returning to their zone with their tails between their legs. It was just over a week later, symbolically on the 4 July 1945, that the Americans finally made it to their sector. They made their base an old Luftwaffe headquarters in the Dahlem Zehlendorf district of south-west Berlin.

on 26 June 1945 – the Republic of China (ROC, Chiang Kai-shek's non-communist Chinese Nationalists) was given the honour of being the first to sign, as they had been the first victim of aggression by an Axis power when Japan invaded Manchuria back in 1931. While the post-First World War League of Nations proved to be a paper tiger, the UN would be a much more powerful forum in the years to come.

Enter the Allies

In the days and weeks that followed Germany's surrender, Allied forces still occupied a third of the territory which would eventually become the Soviet Zone and Churchill was keen to keep hold of it as a bargaining tool until things had settled down a bit and the Soviets

The British made their entry with much less of a fanfare the same day and established their headquarters in the Charlottenburg Wilmersdorf district in the west of Berlin. The British Military Government took over an imposing building overlooking Fehrbelliner Platz and named it Lancaster House (they would not move to the more famous Olympic Park until the early 1950s).[17] The French forces would arrive in August 1945, setting up their headquarters in the Reinickendorf district in the north-west corner of the city.

Although the Soviets had a head start when it came to local and city government, once the other Allies were established in their

Curious Berliners gather around a Sherman tank of the US 2d Armored Division July 1945. (US Army Military History Institute)

US GIs in jeep at the Brandenburg Gate. (US National Archives)

An early success was the agreement on a plan for a move to democratic multi-party government, albeit using more of a decentralised, federalist model (as in the US), with the country split into semi-autonomous States (Länder). They also agreed on an independent judiciary, repealing Hitler's toxic discrimination laws. It is interesting to note that the Soviets were party to these decisions, giving rights and liberties to their vanquished enemies that were not available to their own citizens. Stalin must have sensed some tactical advantage to agreeing with them at the time, as it would not be long before Germans in the Soviet Zone would start to experience Soviet style repression and anything but democratic rule.

The marbled corridors of the Kammergericht would soon, however, echo with sounds of discord, rather than the harmony the EAC had hoped for. Unfortunately, when setting up the Allied Control Council, the EAC made the serious mistake of stipulating that *all* decisions had to be unanimous. Given the souring of relations between the Soviet Union and the other three occupying powers, the ACC was never going to be a very effective organisation, and especially as the Western Allies had been hoodwinked into accepting the unanimous decision clause, the Soviets effectively had a veto over *every* issue. The fact that the Americans and British did not foresee the power the Soviets would yield over the Council either showed extraordinary arrogance on their part, incredible naivety or resigned pragmatism, especially having faced Stalin at the negotiating table numerous times at the various wartime conferences. This would have serious ramifications for the future.

The day to day authority for the city of Berlin, however, lay with the Allied Kommandatura (*Alliierter Kommandantur*), the Four-Power ruling body, in effect a mini version of the Allied Control Council

respective sectors, the official occupation authorities got to work. The ACC took over the very grand former Prussian Kammergericht (Supreme Court) building in the district of Schoenberg and began to govern Germany, initially as a tri-partite organisation; the British, the Americans and the Soviets.

Kammergericht (Supreme Court) building. (Dutch National Archives)

British armoured vehicles pass the reviewing stand in the Charlottenburger Chausee, Berlin, 1945. (Truman Library)

Allied Kommandatura Building. (US Army Military History Institute)

(ACC), which set up on Kaiserwerther Straße in Dahlem. It sat for the first time on 11 July 1945.

Fresh from a hard-fought victory, and in the continuing spirit of wartime cooperation, the British, Americans and French approached the Allied Kommandatura with open minds and a sincere wish to make the Four-Power system work. As such, they unanimously approved all the laws and appointments that the Soviets had made since they entered the city over two months previously, without realising they had been completely stitched up. The Soviets had completely pulled the wool over the eyes of their erstwhile allies.

In this carefully prepared ambush, all the key administrative posts at City Hall had already been filled (mostly by communists) and the city government was already up and running (again, with communists in key positions of power). The Kommandatura shared the same terms of reference as the ACC, so the Soviets were able to use their veto to stop the British, American and French members from removing any of these appointments. The forum quickly descended into a farce.

Outside of the ACC or Kommandatura, from the minute they had arrived, the American, British and French advance parties began to encounter the obstruction, obfuscation and delaying tactics that what would become the norm when dealing with the Soviets. Excuses such as 'we cannot give you an answer because our superiors are away in Moscow', 'sorry, road is closed for mine clearance operations' or 'can't pass because the bridge is unsafe' when it clearly was not, became commonplace as the Soviets started to obstruct and delay their erstwhile allies from taking up their sectors. It had not started well and would soon get much worse.

The British Prime Minister, Winston Churchill, had watched the growth of communism with growing concern. His antipathy dated back to Lenin and the early days of the Russian Revolution, even to the extent of providing materiel to the White Russians during their civil war (although he was responsible for pulling British troops *out* of Russia). He knew what Stalin was up to and could see the 'writing on the wall' for the future of Europe and perhaps the world. It was expedient to enlist Stalin as an ally against Hitler ('the enemy of my enemy is my friend') but it was clear from Yalta onwards that the Grand Alliance would not last past the defeat of Germany. For a while, he even considered invading the Soviet Union (Operation Unthinkable), but Churchill's role in the war was soon brought ignominiously to an end by, of all things, British domestic politics. [18]

The war in Europe was over and Germany was split into four Zones of Occupation, as was the city of Berlin. It was time to focus on bringing the war in the Far East to a swift and successful close. The Big Three met for the third and final time in the Berlin suburb of Potsdam from 17 July to 2 August 1945 for the Potsdam Conference (also known as the Berlin Conference, appropriately codenamed Terminal).[19] Its outcomes would be central to the start of the Cold War and have serious implications for the next four and a half decades.

US C-54s lined up at Gatow having brought the US delegation to the Potsdam Conference, 15 July 1945. (United States Signal Corps via Truman Library)

Churchill inspects a Royal Navy honour guard on arrival at Gatow for the Potsdam Conference, 15 July 1945. (United States Signal Corps via Truman Library)

At flag-raising ceremony in Berlin, Germany, from left to right, General Dwight Eisenhower, General George Patton, and President Harry S. Truman. The Flag of Liberation is being raised over the former Nazi headquarters in Berlin. President Truman is in Germany to attend the Potsdam Conference, 20 July 1945. (United States Army via Truman Library)

Soviet leader, Josef Stalin (second from left), US President Harry S. Truman (foreground, second from right), and British Prime Minister Winston Churchill (right) and their interpreters engage in an informal conversation, prior to the opening of the Potsdam Conference. Admiral William D. Leahy (behind Truman on the left) and Clement Attlee (between Truman and Churchill) are in the background, 17 July 1945. (United States Signal Corps via Truman Library)

Vyacheslav Molotov, with James F. Byrnes and Anthony Eden at the Potsdam Conference, July 1945. (Deutsches Bundesarchiv)

President Harry S. Truman tours Berlin. From left to right (back seat): President Harry S. Truman, Secretary of State James Byrnes, and Admiral William Leahy driving past the ruins of the Reichschancellery in Berlin, where Hitler often spoke from the gallery, 16 July 1945. (United States Signal Corps via Truman Library)

The conference also marked another step change in the global balance of power. The British people went to the polls on 5 July 1945, the first General Election since 1935. When the result was declared on 26 July 1945 and it was a huge shock, nine days into the conference, Winston Churchill – the elder statesman who had led his country to victory – was ousted by Labour leader Clement Atlee in one of the biggest electoral swings of the 20th century.[20] Stalin was amazed that Churchill would let such a thing happen at such a critical moment – a clear example of democracy vs. totalitarianism. All the trust and goodwill that the Allied leaders had built through some very dark times was swept away in an instant. Truman, who was representing his

Allied Leaders at Potsdam Front row: Clement Attlee, Harry S. Truman and Joseph Vissarionovich Stalin. Back row: Admiral William D. Leahy, Ernest Bevin, James F. Byrnes and Vyacheslav Mikhailovich Molotov, July 1945. (Truman Library)

As they all sat down together at Potsdam, the atmosphere must have been electric as the mix of old and new began negotiations on the future shape of Europe. The venue was the Great Hall of the Cecilienhof Palace.[22] Stalin had the table specially made in Moscow and special throne-like armchairs for the three leaders were positioned opposite each other, with ordinary dining chairs squeezed between them for the more senior politicians, diplomats and generals, with translators perched next to the principles and lower level advisors sat on chairs or at small desks in a ring around the outside.

It is obvious with the benefit of hindsight that Stalin was playing mind games with his Allied counterparts. Firstly, the venue he chose was highly symbolic – the home of the eldest child and heir of the *last* German Emperor, Wilhelm II, and the *last* Crown Prince of the German Empire, the Kingdom of Prussia and the Hohenzollern dynasty, a royal line that can be traced back to the 11th century.[23] Secondly, he had chosen a particularly small and claustrophobic room for such an important conference, and the specially commissioned table was remarkably small for the 15 suited or uniformed men squeezed around it. The forced intimacy, claustrophobic environment, and Stalin puffing away on his foul-smelling pipe made for a very tense atmosphere.

Stalin was deeply paranoid and saw enemies everywhere, even from within his so-called allies, fearing capitalist conspiracies to destroy his communist state. He was determined to keep Germany weak, so that it could never rise up and attack the Soviet Union again. The discussions were characterised by inflexibility, recrimination, mistrust and obfuscation, sorely lacking in the cooperation and compromise that was instrumental in the Allies coming together to defeat Nazism. The orderly work undertaken by the EAC and the progress made in the various conferences right up to Yalta earlier that year, gave in to a series of *faits accomplis* and very uncomfortable compromises.

country in his first international summit following the death of FDR, and new British Prime Minister Attlee had some very big shoes to fill.

At the same time, Churchill's debonair Foreign Secretary, Eton and Oxford educated Anthony Eden, was replaced by veteran trade unionist Ernest Bevin – the contrast could not have been greater. At least Truman's newly appointed Secretary of State James Byrnes offered some continuity, having accompanied Roosevelt to Yalta.[21]

Crucially, the negotiators from the Soviet Union had remained a constant in all the Big Three meetings, in fact, Molotov had been involved right back to the first Moscow Conference (codenamed Caviar) in September 1941. The Soviet Foreign Minister Vyacheslav Molotov was a wily old Bolshevik with impeccable revolutionary credentials. As a member of the Petrograd Military Revolutionary Committee (MILREVCOM), he had helped plan the October Revolution in 1917 and had survived Stalin's bloody rise to power to become his right-hand man, going on to sign the controversial but ill-fated Molotov-Ribbentrop Pact in 1939.

The Soviets had had Berlin to themselves since the Red Army entered the city in April and had used that time to their advantage – as the British and American delegations arrived, they were greeted with huge posters of Stalin, Lenin and Marx hanging from buildings and monuments.

Portrait of Stalin on a monument alongside a row of burnt-out buildings on Unter den Linden, Berlin, 16 July 1945. (Richard Beckman via Truman Library)

Cecilienhof Palace in Potsdam, Germany, venue for the Potsdam Conference, July 1945. (US Navy via Truman Library)

The Opening Session of the Potsdam Conference poses for photographers. Clockwise from Churchill: Prime Minister Winston Churchill; Unidentified British officer; British Leader of the Opposition Clement Attlee; unidentified Soviet officer; Soviet Foreign Minister Vyacheslav Molotov; Joseph Stalin; Unidentified Soviet Officer; Unidentified Soviet; Admiral William D. Leahy; Secretary of State James Byrnes; President Truman: Charles Bohlen; two unidentified men; British Foreign Secretary Anthony Eden, 17 July 1945. (US National Archives)

The subject of reparations became a major sticking point between the Soviets and the two Western powers. Back at Yalta, Roosevelt had agreed to Stalin's demands for $10 billion worth of reparations (50 percent of the arbitrary figure of $20 billion agreed at the conference). Stalin had argued for it as compensation for the tremendous destruction and losses as a result of Hitler's invasion, and Roosevelt was of a mind to agree if it meant that the Soviets would join the war against Japan and also participate in Roosevelt's grand plan for the United Nations. However, Roosevelt's successor, Harry Truman, did not share FDR's generosity and forced the point that reparations could *only* be 'extracted' from the victorious power's *own* Zones of Occupation. Reparations for Poland were also to come out of the Soviet Zone. The declaration did, however, allow for a degree of bartering: in return for commodities such as grain, minerals, and coal from within the Soviet Zone, the Soviets could claim industrial capital equipment from the Western zones. [24]

Truman was very keen to avoid a repeat of the Treaty of Versailles and was keen that the German economy should be allowed to produce enough to allow exports, earning revenue to maintain a tolerable standard of living. The Potsdam Declaration went as far to state that the post-war German economy should be able to keep the occupying

forces supplied, provide for the huge numbers of displaced persons arriving from all over Europe and maintain a standard of living for its citizens 'not to exceed the average standard of living in Europe (excl. UK and USSR).'

The Soviets went on to strip the zone that would become East Germany of most of its infrastructure, leaving it woefully undercapitalised and highly dependent on the Soviet Union, thus hastening the division of Germany and fuelling the Cold War for decades to come.

The Conference Protocols demanded the complete disarmament, demilitarisation and de-Nazification of Germany and dismantling of all supporting industry, thus preventing any possible resurgence of militarism or Nazism. The de-Nazification process also decided how to go about prosecuting German war criminals, which would lead to the Nuremberg Trials, the formation of the International Court of Justice (under the auspices of the UN), the International War Crimes Tribunals and the International Criminal Court.

Although West Germany would go on to become the economic powerhouse of Europe, the Allied leader's initial intentions were modest. As well as providing for the occupying powers and displaced persons as stated above, the plan was for the economy to be decentralised to avoid concentrations of power and influence and focussed on agriculture and peaceful domestic industries. However, the decision about reconstituting a national German government was postponed indefinitely, with the responsibility of running the country passed to the Four-Power ACC.

Mindful of what was to come in only a few short years, two of the provisions of the declaration have particular resonance:

> So far as is practicable, there shall be uniformity of treatment of the German population throughout Germany.

> Subject to the necessity for maintaining military security, freedom of speech, press and religion shall be permitted, and religious institutions shall be respected. Subject likewise to the maintenance of military security, the formation of free trade unions shall be permitted.

The Trinity explosion, taken 0.053 seconds after detonation, New Mexico, USA, 16 July 1945. (Los Alamos National Laboratory)

It is interesting to reflect on just how far the Soviet Zone, which of course became East Germany, deviated from this high-minded starting position almost as soon as it was signed.

Stalin also made a big win over Poland, which was a key building block in his grand plan for a strong buffer zone between Western Europe (Germany mainly) and the Motherland. He successfully argued that the Curzon Line should remain as his western border with a newly 'liberated' Poland, thus holding on to the land he acquired from Poland back in 1939. As consolation, the Poles were assigned a huge chunk of eastern Germany, effectively 'moving' Poland 250km (150 miles) to the west. Stalin then went about imposing his will (and ideology) over occupied Poland in his usual fashion. The conference did, however, hold back on confirming the border between Germany and this 'new' Poland (the 'Oder-Neisse line'), pending resolution of the German peace settlement.[25] Through his iron will and brute force, Stalin had managed to secure the most important piece in his 'Ring of Steel', all with the thin veneer of international acceptance.

The Potsdam Conference would also be responsible for several other globally significant moments in the build-up to the Cold War, the most notable being a quiet aside Truman made to Stalin on 24 July 1945. Just before the conference began, the US had successfully tested an atomic bomb in the New Mexico desert. The test was codenamed Trinity and was the culmination of an extraordinary top secret scientific and engineering effort codenamed the Manhattan Project. At 05:29 on 16 July 1945, the world changed forever, as the power within the atom had finally been released in a huge radioactive explosion.

After the successful Trinity Test on 16 July, Truman felt inclined to hint at what they had achieved, and let Stalin know that they had successfully tested a special weapon; 'a new weapon of unusual destructive force', although he did not identify it as an atomic bomb per

se.[26] Stalin appeared particularly unimpressed, which baffled Truman. Thinking it would strengthen his negotiating position with Stalin, he was unaware that Stalin knew all about the bomb via his spies within the Manhattan Project. Stalin had in fact known about the bomb for much longer than Truman![27] He told Truman that 'he was glad to hear it and hoped that we would make good use of it against the Japanese'. This low-key conversation, with its unprecedented global implications, heralded the era of Atomic Diplomacy, with the bomb becoming inextricably linked to East-West relations.

As far as the split of Berlin was concerned, the Soviets claimed that the destruction in their sector of the city was so great that the French sector would have to come out of the British and American sectors, just as they insisted for the occupation zones of Germany. On 26 July 1945, the agreement defining the French Zone of Occupation in Germany was signed, with the French having a place on the Kommandatura in Berlin, and over the next few months the British and American inter-sector borders were adjusted to make room for a French sector in the north of the city, with the United States keeping transit rights across French territory.[28] Controversially, the French were not invited to participate in the Potsdam Conference, which Charles de Gaulle resented for the rest of his life.

By Potsdam, the EAC had successfully run its course, bringing together four headstrong nations in the midst of war, but with a shared common purpose (that is, the defeat of the Nazis) which helped overcome most of the barriers. The personal relationships of the civil servants and military representatives that had built over time helped water down any extreme views from their respective governments and also helped head off any misunderstandings that could have had serious consequences. It is sad that the spirit of wartime cooperation was to quickly disappear, particularly by the Soviets, as soon as their common enemy had been defeated. With its job completed, the EAC was officially dissolved at Potsdam.

The Americans and British issued a proclamation to the leaders of Japan, demanding their unconditional surrender (the Soviet Union was still officially neutral in the war against Japan, so they were not party to this ultimatum). They soundly rejected the Potsdam terms on 29 July 1945 and sealed their fate.

A New World

The world's first atomic attack took place on 6 August 1945 over the Japanese city of Hiroshima, with the second following on 9 August 1945 over Nagasaki. In the meantime, Stalin had fulfilled his Yalta pledge of invading the Japanese puppet state of Manchukuo in north-eastern China, which was previously known as Manchuria.[29] The combination of the Soviet's major push on Japan's western flank and the devastation of two atomic bombs pushed Emperor Hirohito to finally accept the terms of the Potsdam Conference (unconditional surrender, in all but name) on 15 August 1945, which became known as VJ (Victory over Japan) Day.[30] The Japanese formal surrender took place on USS *Missouri* on 2 September 1945. The Second World War had officially come to an end.

However, if the bombs on Hiroshima and Nagasaki were the *last* shots of the Second World War, they were also arguably the *first* shots of the Cold War. The dropping of the atomic bombs on Japan was a watershed moment on many levels, ending the Second World War, but also heralding the start of a new world conflict that would become known as the Cold War. If the world was in any doubt, two key speeches from either side of the great ideological divide confirmed it within weeks of each other.

On 9 February 1946, Stalin spoke to a packed audience of party loyalists at the Bolshoi Theatre in Moscow. He was there ostensibly to deliver a speech to a group of 'voters' to help secure his 're-election', and it is therefore become known as his 'Election Speech'.[31] In typically bombastic style, he extolled the virtues of the communist system and lambasted all aspects of the capitalist system, clearly heralding the end of the Grand Alliance between his wartime allies – divorce on the grounds of 'irreconcilable differences'. He blamed the capitalist system for the war that ravaged his nation and killed some 20 million of his people. Citing Marxist doctrine, he predicted the inevitable breakdown of capitalism through economic and militaristic crises and reminded his adoring audience that communism was inherently superior and would ultimately prevail (just as Marx had predicted). George Kennan's famous 'Long Telegram' to the US leadership followed on 22 February 1946, confirming the view that communism (or perhaps Stalinism) was the mortal enemy of the free world.

A few weeks later, Winston Churchill, now Leader of the Opposition, returned to the United States to deliver a speech at Westminster College in Fulton, Missouri. For many historians, his 5 March 1946 'Sinews of Peace' speech heralded the start of the Cold War and it has become famous for coining the phrases 'Special Relationship' and 'Iron Curtain'. Churchill believed the 'Special Relationship' between the British and Americans had been central to winning the war against Germany and Japan and was crucial to winning the new peace:

> Neither the sure prevention of war, nor the continuous rise of world organisation will be gained without what I have called the fraternal association of the English-speaking peoples. This means a *special relationship* between the British Commonwealth and Empire and the United States.[32]

Despite being an uneven relationship, it stood the test of time and outlasted the Cold War. The section of the speech concerning 'the present position in Europe' was particularly prescient and gave the world the idea of Stalin's 'Iron Curtain':[33]

> From Stettin in the Baltic to Trieste in the Adriatic, an *iron curtain* has descended across the Continent. Behind that line lie all the capitals of the ancient states of Central and Eastern Europe. Warsaw, Berlin, Prague, Vienna, Budapest, Belgrade, Bucharest and Sofia, all these famous cities and the populations around them lie in what I must call the Soviet sphere, and all are subject in one form or another, not only to Soviet influence but to a very high and, in many cases, increasing measure of control from Moscow.[34]

So, whichever date is chosen for the start of the Cold War: the Potsdam Conference; the dropping of the atomic bombs over Japan in August 1945; Stalin's 'Election' Speech in February 1946; or Churchill's Iron Curtain Speech in March 1946, the world was once again facing global conflict and with the arrival of nuclear weapons, the future was clouded by a new and existential threat.

3
THE GRIP TIGHTENS

As the world came to terms with the new atomic age, Stalin quickly got to work in shoring up the 'Ring of Steel' that was going to protect Russia from further invasion. His 'Iron Curtain' was almost complete, with Poland, Czechoslovakia, Hungary and Romania forming a chain from the Baltic to the Black Sea, occupied by his Red Army and in the process of being transformed into satellite states of the Soviet Union. The last piece in the jigsaw was eastern Germany, which was the gateway to the flat plains of northern Europe and onwards to Moscow. He held the territory seized by the Red Army in the closing months of the war and also allocated to him by the EAC as his Zone of Occupation.

Unlike the other satellite states, where he could do what he wanted with no outside interference, he had to be careful with eastern Germany because of the unusual Four-Power agreements with his fellow allies.

He also had to contend with the irritation of having a Western enclave right in the middle of his zone in the form of West Berlin. With the Western Powers constantly looking over his shoulder, he needed to build a 'legitimate' power base to ensure his north-western flank was completely secure. It was time to engineer a political coup d'état in his zone.

Since entering the city of Berlin in April 1945, the groundwork for this coup had been underway. German communist Walter Ulbricht and his colleagues had been deployed to slowly and deliberately throw a communist net over the city, its administration, its infrastructure and its social and cultural life. Now it was time to tackle mainstream politics.

The Soviets were keen to restart political activity in their zone, albeit under close supervision. The German Communist Party, the

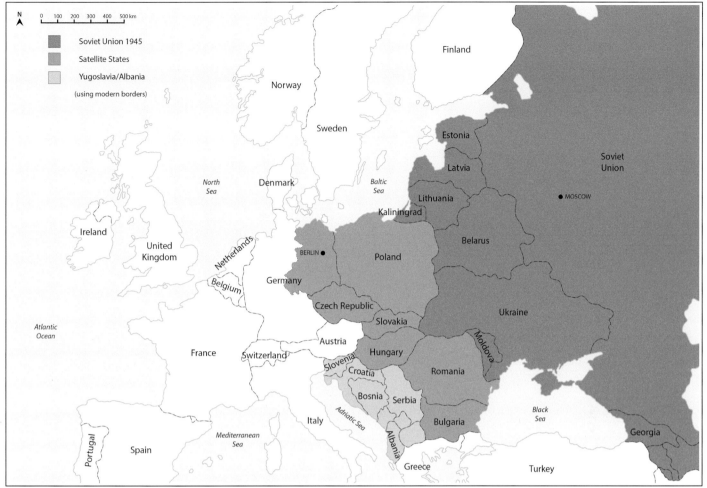

Soviet sphere of influence 1945. By 1945, Stalin had virtually completed his 'Ring of Steel' and his troops had 'liberated' almost all of Eastern Europe. Leningrad and his north-west flank had been secured after the Finnish Winter War in 1939 and for the moment, Yugoslavia under Marshall Tito was following the Soviet model (they would diverge in 1948). See his progress compared to the map on page 7. (George Anderson)

The public faces behind East German politics in 1945. Otto Grothewohl (SPD), Andreas Hermes (CDU), Wilhelm Pieck (KPD), Dr. Arthur Werner, (Oberbürgermeister Berlin), Waldemar Koch (LDPD), 1945. Real power, however, rested with Walter Ulbricht, not shown in this photo. (Deutsche Fotothek)

KPD had been re-formed in the weeks after VE Day but in order to give the appearance of democracy, the Soviets also permitted the Social Democratic Party of Germany (*Sozialdemokratische Partei Deutschlands* or SPD) to reform in the Soviet Zone, with veteran socialist Otto Grotewohl at the helm. The British, French and American Zones were less of a hurry, but under Kurt Schumacher, the SPD began activity again in the West, albeit without official approval.[1] Both arms of the party thrived, and despite an acute shortage of paper to produce posters and party literature, the SPD quickly became the most popular left-leaning party in post-war Germany, considerably outstripping the KPD in the Soviet Zone. In political circles, it was generally assumed that the SPD would go on to govern across all of the occupation zones, when the occupying powers permitted it.

Schumacher rejected Grotewohl's overtures for closer collaboration with the KPD and the two arms of the party started to head in different directions. In the West, Schumacher's party grew, but began to struggle against a growing anti-socialist backlash across western Germany (encouraged and supported by the Americans). This allowed Konrad Adenauer, the former mayor of Cologne, and his Christian Democratic Union (CDU) to gain popularity, uniting many pre-war German conservatives into his new party.[2]

In the Soviet Zone, the Soviet Military Administration (SMA) began a carefully orchestrated campaign to control the political scene. In July 1945, they forced *all* East German political parties to join the 'Unity Front of the Anti-Fascist Democratic Parties', an anti-fascist bloc comprising Ulbricht's German Communist Party (KPD), Grotewohl's Social Democratic Party of Germany (SPD), the centre-right Christian Democratic Union (CDU) and the Liberal Democratic Party (LDPD).[3] This (very) broad church of political opinions had little in common apart from a desire to see Germany rise from the ashes, but in order to operate, they had to become part of this 'Unity' or 'National' Front.

It quickly became clear to the SMA that the KPD was not going to become the party of choice across the Soviet Zone without a bit of help. They knew that the KPD needed the SPD, and to a lesser extent the other parties, to 'carry' them to pseudo-democratic legitimacy and from as early as September 1945, the SMA began to exert pressure

Unsubtle KPD propaganda accusing Kurt Schumacher, the leader of the West German arm of the SPD, of being a 'Quisling', a traitor. It also criticises Ernst Reuter, the Mayor of West Berlin and Carl-Hubert Schwennicke, leader of the West Berlin offshoot of the LDPD, 1946. (Charles E. Steinheimer via Albert Grandolini)

The handshake between Wilhelm Pieck (KPD) and Otto Grotewohl (SPD) that created the SED, at the Admiralspalast (Metropoltheater) in Friedrichstrasse, 21 April 1946. Note Walter Ulbricht on the right-hand side – the man who had engineered the merger on behalf of his Soviet masters. Erich Honecker can be seen on the third row, second from the left. (Deutsche Fotothek)

on the SPD to merge their (more popular) party with the (less popular) KPD. As it was, the KPD was the only party who had the ear of the SMA and so they were the only ones with real power in the newly created Berlin Assembly.

The first real test came in November 1945 in the elections to the National Council in neighbouring Austria, where the KPD was soundly defeated by the main pre-war parties. The SMA were not prepared to take any chances in their Zone of Occupation and began to increase the pressure on the SPD to merge. This was done through propaganda and political lobbying, but when the SPD hesitated, the Soviets resorted to physical intimidation by arresting key SPD members. It is estimated that some 20,000 Social Democrats were targeted between December 1945 and April 1946, with many imprisoned and some even killed.

Operating across the four occupation zones, the SPD quickly began to pull itself apart: the members in the Soviet Zone under Otto Grotewohl swung towards the extreme left and communism, while Kurt Schumacher in the western zones argued for more a more mainstream form of socialism.[4]

What followed was a classic example of Soviet political manoeuvring. When a cross-Germany meeting of the SPD in January 1946 comprehensively rejected merging with the KPD, the SMA refused to let news of the decision be reported to SPD members within their zone. In March, the Soviets then refused to allow a referendum of Berlin members to be held in their sector of the city.

Formation of the SED

It was becoming obvious that the SMA could not win over rank-and-file members of the SPD through conventional means, so Stalin forced the issue, imposing a merger on the two parties. On

Logo of the Sozialistische Einheitspartei Deutschlands, the SED, featuring the famous handshake. (Public domain)

21 April 1946, at a set-piece rally in the theatre at the old Admiralspalast building on Friedrichstrasse, the joint leaders; Wilhelm Pieck (KPD) and Otto Grotewohl (SPD), came on stage from opposite sides and symbolically shook hands in the middle. The Socialist Unity Party of Germany (*Sozialistische Einheitspartei Deutschlands* or SED) was born, and their handshake was immortalised in the SED logo and flag.

Their deputies were Walter Ulbricht (KPD) and Max Fechner (SPD) although the real power lay with Ulbricht because of his links with the SMA. Initially, the newly elected committees were composed of equal numbers of Social Democrats and Communists, but very quickly the Social Democrats were side-lined forced out by widespread communist intimidation. The new party brought together approximately 1.3 million members, with around 46 percent of them coming from the KPD. Despite being in the minority, the SED was the dominant force thanks to their links with the SMA, holding a veto over any proposal from the other parties that was not in line with SED policies.

Part of the negotiations to merge the parties included discussions on the merger of their newspapers, and the result was *Neues Deutschland* (or *New Germany*), which was launched on 23 April 1946 as the official paper of the SED. At the time, newspapers were still an essential communication tool, used extensively for propaganda purposes. The first print run was 400,000 and it fed party content to the East German population for the next four decades. Apart from listening illegally to Western radio, there was no real news alternative, so the party line was the *only* story received by the average East German.[5]

Very soon the leaderships of the various 'opposition' parties within the Unity Front were purged and replaced by new leaders who were sympathetic to the SED. They swiftly became 'opposition' in name only.

In October 1946, despite a Soviet controlled press and widespread voter intimidation, the SED did badly in local elections right across the Soviet Zone.[6] The SPD won an overall majority in the new Berlin city assembly but struggled to govern in the face of Soviet stalling tactics and their veto within the Allied Kommandatura, which stopped the SPD ousting communists from the key positions.[7]

Stalin was working to a tried-and-tested formula. As soon as the Red Army had taken the city back in April 1945, the Soviet Military Administration embarked on a 'Hearts and Minds' campaign trying to make living in the city more tolerable. Having then stitched up the political scene in their Zone of Occupation, they went about attempting to dominate every other aspect of society.

The SMA had taken control of newspapers and publishing immediately after entering Berlin, but they needed to exert their influence over East Germany's young generation, the future citizens of Ulbricht's socialist paradise. The Soviets frowned upon the International Scout Movement, set up in Great Britain by Lord Baden Powell before the First World War, as some Russian Scouts sided with the White Russians against the Bolsheviks during the Revolution. The Young Pioneers were therefore created in 1922 as a communist version of Scouting and they became a core part of Soviet Society. Following this model (and disturbingly, that of the Hitler Youth in Nazi Germany), the SED set up an umbrella state-controlled youth organisation to catch their future citizens while they were young and impressionable. They began with the *Freie Deutsche Jugend* (Free German Youth or FDJ) as the official youth movement in the Soviet Zone on 7 March 1946, having laid the foundations with the anti-fascist youth committees set up in the Soviet Zone of Occupation in June 1945.

The FDJ was the only officially recognised and funded youth organisation in East Germany and at its peak in the early 80s, it had 2.3 million members, representing 75 percent of the population aged between 14 and 25. The FDJ was to be found everywhere; in all schools, universities, factories and businesses and was highly politicised, with its members being regularly used for 'spontaneous' demonstrations in support of the latest policy from the SED. Unsurprisingly, the FDJ was a major feeder into the DDR's armed forces.

On 13 December 1948, the FDJ created the *Pionierorganisation Ernst Thälmann* to extend their reach all the way down to primary school children. Named after the leader of the KPD who was imprisoned by the National Socialists and executed in 1944 at Buchenwald Concentration Camp, they created the *Jungen Pionieren* (Young Pioneers) which covered the ages six to ten. The children would then move on to the *Thälmann Pionieren* (Thälmann Pioneers), which went from ten to 14, which was old enough to join the FDJ proper. This system allowed for the systematic indoctrination of East Germany's youth from the age of six right up to 25. [8]

It is impossible to avoid uncomfortable comparisons here with Nazi Germany: military style uniforms, marching, saluting, flags, banners, torchlight parades and carefully choreographed pageantry, less than a decade after the end of the war and theoretically at the opposite end of the political spectrum. All sport, cultural life, further and higher education and even choice of career was controlled by the FDJ and as such, if you were not a member, you were very much on the fringes of East German society. From 1947 to 1990, *Junge Welt*, the official newspaper of the FDJ was produced, with up to 1.5 million copies being printed daily.

For the working population, the SED created the *Freie Deutsche Gewerkschaftsbund* (Federation of Free German Trade Unions or FDGB), an umbrella trade organisation representing a number of individual trade unions, founded in February 1946. As with many Soviet backed initiatives, the FDGB gave the appearance of a freely organised labour movement, but in reality, from the late 1940s, it was completely controlled by the SED. Whilst membership was voluntary, as with the FDJ, you had to be a member if you wanted any form of career and the FDGB came to be a core element of the East German state, with representatives in the Volkskammer and Politburo. And for the women of eastern Germany, the SED created the *Demokratische Frauen-bund Deutschlands* (Women's Democratic League of Germany or DFD), which provided a voice for women's issues in the Soviet

FDJ Broadcast Concert. (Deutsche Fotothek)

East Berlin Police struggle with a Berlin photographer when he tries to cross the border from East Berlin to West Berlin. (Truman Library)

The Freie Deutsche Jugend (Free German Youth or FDJ) badge (Private collection.

covert raids over sector borders to seize known troublemakers in the Western sectors, who mistakenly thought they were under the protection of the British, French or Americans.

By mid-1946, the SMA had built the foundations of an extensive paramilitary structure, which would remain in the eastern zone of Germany until the fall of the Berlin Wall. On 30 July 1946, the SED (on instructions from the SMA) set up the German Administration of the Interior (the *Deutsche Verwaltung des Innern* or DVdI) to coordinate and control law and order. A communist German auxiliary police force had been established in the Soviet Zone soon after VE Day, which was organised into the *Deutsche Volkspolizei* (German People's Police or DVP), a.k.a. the *Volkspolizei* (or VP) or colloquially as the VoPos.

In 1948, the SMA created an additional paramilitary force called the *Bereitschaftspolizei* (Alert Police). These 'Barracked' or 'Garrisoned' police were organised and equipped as light infantry, with uniforms and weapons supplied by the Soviets. Controversially, many of their recruits were former Wehrmacht POWs, who had received ideological training in Soviet prison camps before being repatriated to the Soviet

Occupation Zone and provided support and counselling with an SED approved agenda.

The Soviet backed SED was remarkably successful in taking control of society in the Soviet Occupation Zone within a few months of the defeat of the Nazis. Using tried-and-tested methods, they took over the media and organised the youth, the labour force and the women of eastern Germany, all under a communist banner. Beginning as a 'hearts and minds' campaign, the thin veneer of civility would soon wear through as the iron grip tightened. All these were the building blocks of the communist state which would go on to rule eastern Germany for the next 40 years or so.

Beginnings of a Militarised Police State

The Soviet's control over local government gave them a veneer of respectability, but SMA and their German lackies soon began a crackdown on dissidents across the Soviet Zone, with hundreds being taken into custody. They even conducted

FDJ march in Berlin carrying a banner with the slogan 'Long live Stalin, the best friend of the German people!', June 1950 (Charles E. Steinheimer via Albert Grandolini)

The Kasernierte Volkspolizei (KVP), or 'Barracked' People's Police was the precursor to the National People's Army (NVA) in East Germany. (Charles E. Steinheimer via Albert Grandolini)

the DVdI became the Ministry of the Interior (*Ministerium des Innern* or MdI).

The final paramilitary force in the structure was the elite *Grenztruppen der DDR* (Border Troops of the DDR), who were responsible for policing the border between East and West Germany and also would be a key component of the infamous Berlin Wall. They were set up by the SMA in December 1946 as the *Deutsche Grenzpolizei* (German Border Police) and went through various iterations before becoming the *Grenztruppen der DDR* in 1961, along with the construction of the Wall. These 'political' paramilitary forces were key tools in controlling the German population in the Soviet Zone and were the first stages in the development of the East German security state.

The SMA employed another well proven technique to dominate the population – they required *all* workers in their zone to register with the authorities, which was a pre-requisite for rations and employment. This pseudo-census would have several benefits; it would identify anybody 'useful' to the Soviets authorities, it would flush out or isolate dissidents and would also identify a general labour force that could be employed as they saw fit. Part of the reparations deal thrashed out at Yalta and Potsdam allowed for the transfer of labour from Germany to start rebuilding the Soviet Union, but the SMA went about it on an epic scale.

Zone. Many of their generals were Hitler's former generals, deliberately placed in positions of authority, thus preserving and continuing the spirit of German and Prussian martial traditions, their 'tried-and-tested' principles of military drills and even the external appearance and behaviour patterns of German militarism. The force was quickly put under the control the DVdI and went through a number of organisational and name changes, before becoming the *Kasernierte Volkspolizei* (KVP) in 1952. On the foundation of the DDR in 1949,

East German Volkspolizei armed with Sturmgewehr (StG) 44 assault rifles. (Albert Grandolini)

Trooper from the Deutsche Grenzpolizei armed with a MPi41 submachine gun. The MPi41 was the East German designation of the Soviet PPSh-41. (Albert Grandolini)

The deportees included known troublemakers, dissidents and criminals, including former Nazi party members, bureaucrats, intellectuals and anyone considered a threat by the Soviets.[9] They also included hundreds of thousands of ordinary Germans, who found themselves on trains en route to factories and labour camps all over the Soviet Union, joining German POWs and political prisoners. They would be put to work in reconstruction projects, in heavy industry and in labour-intensive or dangerous occupations such as uranium mining. The work regimes were brutal and living conditions appalling, with as many as 40 percent of them dying in the camps from illness or malnutrition or being deliberately killed by guards or other inmates. Some would spend decades in the Soviet Gulag system before eventually being allowed home, while others were simply listed as 'missing'. The parallels with the mass expulsion of European Jews by trains to the concentration camps of Eastern Europe are of course unmistakable.

Although 'Forced Labour' had been agreed as a form of reparation, when the Western Allies discovered the fate of these deportees, they protested vigorously via the Allied Control Commission but as the Soviets held a veto over any action, the deportations continued unhindered. The reparations process during the rest of 1945 and into 1946, had the effect of 'importing' skills not previously held in the Soviet Union, acquiring a substantial mobile slave labour force, while at the same time, ridding their occupation zone of dissent.

The West take the initiative

Stalin and Ulbricht may have been very busy in the Soviet Zone, but the Western Allies had not been standing still. The British Military Government, in the form of the Control Commission Germany (British Element), abbreviated to CCG (BE), set up their headquarters in Bad Oeynhausen, which is between Hannover and Osnabruck.[10] Immediately after VE Day, it was headed by Field Marshal Bernard Law Montgomery, 1st Viscount Montgomery of Alamein, a.k.a. 'Monty', who had spearheaded the British advance into Germany. He handed over to Air Chief Marshall Sir Sholto Douglas in 1946, who in turn handed over to General Sir Brian Robertson in 1947, who had very capably served as both Montgomery's and Douglas's deputy.[11]

Planning for the administration of a conquered Germany had begun early in the war, in parallel with the work the EAC and ACC were doing. Following the invasion of Europe in June 1944, British and Canadian troops under Montgomery fought their way across the northern plains of Europe, pushing the Germans back, and in March 1945 succeeded in crossing the Rhine.[12] The advancing troops were closely followed by teams of Civil Affairs officers, who took over the administration of towns and cities that had been overrun by the Allied forces.

Following a well-rehearsed plan, a basic team comprised:

- 2 Generalist Officers (representing the various Divisions and Branches of the CCG(BE))
- 2 Public Safety Officers (Police)
- 2 Clerks (with one being an interpreter)
- 1 Cook
- 1 Batman[13]
- 2 Drivers

Depending on the size of town or scale of the problem, they had to be supplemented with further administrative, finance, supply, medical or transport staff, and would occupy whatever former local government premises they could find.

Control Commission Germany (British Element) Formation Patch Badge. (Private collection)

Control Commission Germany (British Element) Cap Badge. (Private collection)

Control Commission Germany (British Element) Public Safety Branch Cap Badge. (Private collection)

A number of unique organisations came together to administer post-war Occupied Germany. One was the Public Safety Branch, who were effectively the military government's civilian police force. They were recruited by the Home Office mostly from the various police forces around the UK and their experience and common-sense approach to policing helped rebuild the German people's trust in their police. Their structure mirrored the constabularies from back home, with CID (Criminal Investigations Department), Special Branch, training and headquarters functions with links to health and fire services.

Many of the cities they arrived in were little more than ruins, with an atmosphere akin to the old Wild West. Gangs of armed criminals, mostly former POWs or forced labourers, roamed the streets in a free-for-all of looting, rape and murder. General Robertson described the role of the Civil Affairs teams as a 'Policeman taking control of the scene of an accident', which seems very appropriate. Soldiers accompanying the teams were ordered to shoot on sight when confronted by the looters.

Their role changed over time, but initially they had the grim task of dealing with the thousands of dead bodies that were littering the streets or buried under rubble. Then there were millions of Displaced Persons (DP), who needed to be processed and if appropriate, repatriated home, with careful checks to weed out any war criminals as part of the de-Nazification process. Many of these DPs had been brutalised by years of war, which made policing them a real challenge. The black market was another problem, and the Public Safety Officers led crackdowns ranging from small time dealing to large scale racketeering and organised crime. The wider role of the Military Government had a key role to play here, working to restore normal economic conditions with the restoration of German industry, currency reforms and implementation of the European Recovery Plan (Marshall Plan).

The CCG(BE) also played a key role in the establishment of the post-war German police force and independent judiciary. The Legal Branch recruited, trained and swore in new judges, who were not tainted with associations with the former Nazi regime, while the Public Safety Branch began working on creating a new German police force for the British Zone of West Germany. Recruits were carefully vetted, weeding out any with criminal or Nazi pasts, and training schools were set up all over the zone. With intensive training and mentoring from the former British 'Bobbies', they were moulded into a trustworthy policing service, that were 'servants of the public, not their master', undoing years of Nazi tyranny. In stark contrast to the Third Reich, they also recruited women police officers, who would be particularly useful in tackling the scourge of prostitution and countless orphaned street children. The new German police force was deliberately decentralised to avoid any chance of it becoming the tool of a political party again.

Another arm of the CCG(BE) was the British Frontier Service (BFS), which monitored the borders between Germany and her immediate neighbours. Their initial focus was on the borders with Belgium, Denmark and the Netherlands but following the 1948 Berlin blockade, they increasingly focussed on the long border between West and East Germany, which would become the 'Inner German Border'. The Service was staffed by former British military personnel, and while they were civilians, they were given honorary Army ranks and wore a distinctive dark blue naval style uniform, designed by their first Director, who happened to be a Royal Navy Officer. Their duties included anti-smuggling patrols, helping British military personnel and their families when transiting across the DDR

Corp of Royal Military Police Cap Badge. (Private collection)

to West Berlin, providing guides for visiting VIPs, liaising with the fledgling West German police and customs services and helping to defuse any border incidents – they would regularly accompany British Army patrols along sensitive parts of the border.[14]

Wherever troops go, they are accompanied by Military Police and Occupied Germany was no exception. The Corps of Royal Military Police (also known as RMP or the 'Redcaps' because of the bright red covers on their caps) had a strong presence across the British Zone, working alongside the British Civil Authorities.[15] Their responsibility was to investigate crime within the British Forces community stationed in numerous locations across West Germany. Like their civilian counterparts in the CID, the Special Investigation Branch (SIB) investigated the more serious criminal and military offences. Redcaps in Occupied Germany had the extra challenge of working alongside both British and German civilian authorities and operating in a very complex and dangerous environment.

An M20 Utility Car leading M8 Greyhound armoured cars of the US Constabulary on patrol in the American Zone. (Albert Grandolini)

Trooper from the US Constabulary armed with an M1 Garand rifle. (Albert Grandolini)

Trooper from the US Constabulary shows his M3 submachine gun (minus its magazine) to his Soviet counterpart. He is also armed with a M1911 pistol. The Soviet soldier is armed with a PPsH submachine gun. (Albert Grandolini)

In Berlin, the RMP had the additional role of liaising with their counterparts in the American, French and Soviet sectors and all the political sensitivities that brought. 247 (Berlin) Provost Company, 2 Regiment, Corps of Royal Military Police were stationed at the Olympic Stadium in the city and maintained a very high profile, ensuring that Great Britain's Four-Power rights were maintained.[16]

The American garrison in Berlin was policed by Military Policemen (MPs) of the 287th Military Police Company, who operated around the city on foot, in jeeps and even on horseback. A separate organisation, the US Constabulary, was created in July 1946 to concentrate on policing the occupation throughout the whole American Zone, a task normal US infantry was not well suited to. It was created as a highly mobile mechanized elite force using armoured cars, tanks, jeeps, motorcycles and other vehicles outfitted with full radio and signal equipment, plus horse-mounted troops for riot control.

They wore a distinctive uniform and were known as the 'Circle C Cowboys' after their highly polished helmets with a blue stripe sandwiched between two bright yellow stripes going around the helmet, with the Constabulary insignia, a big 'C' in a circle on the front. The Germans called them the 'Lightning Police' after the lightning bolt on their shoulder flash. As well as being heavily armed, they had additional powers over normal MPs.[17]

The French maintained a paramilitary Gendarmerie unit within Berlin, closely liaising with their British and American colleagues.

It was becoming very clear to the British and American occupying powers that the way Germany had been divided was hampering the recovery and rehabilitation of the conquered country, and with it the recovery of Europe as a whole. In particular, the division was causing considerable economic difficulties; 'raw materials [were separated] from processors, manufacturers from markets and farm regions from industrial areas'. Anything the British or Americans proposed for closer integration was vetoed by the Soviets in the ACC so by mid-1946, they had made little progress, in fact, the division of Germany was even greater than it was at Potsdam.

The Americans had begun a degree of integration within their zone, by creating a Länderrat or Council of States, which at least devolved some limited powers to the individual States in their zone. There was no sign that the impasse at the ACC was going to change so on 20 July 1946, at the 34th meeting of the ACC, the US extended an invitation to the other Allied powers to take steps in the direction of establishing some form of economic unity.

The US government had authorised its representatives on the Allied Control Council to join with the representatives of any other occupying power or powers in measures for the treatment of their respective zones as an economic unit, pending quadripartite agreement which would permit the application of the Potsdam decision to treat all of Germany as an economic unit so as to attempt a balanced economy throughout Germany.

Unsurprisingly, the Soviets declined to join the coalition, but more tellingly, so did the French. The French proved to be rather difficult bedfellows, coming to the table with a very different set of objectives. De Gaulle was paranoid that if the Germans were allowed to re-establish a central government, this could lead to a new European power base that could threaten the new peace (understandable, given France had been invaded by Germany three times in the previous 70 years). He wanted to see a decentralised federal government and Allied control of the major industrial centres of Germany. This was one of the early examples of Paris's single-minded approach, which continued through much of the Cold War. The British were the only ones to take up the offer and on 30 July 1946, a Bizonal structure and organisation was agreed on. They agreed to adopt a common standard of living, a common consumer ration, and pool all resources across the new territory to be allocated to the individual states as required.

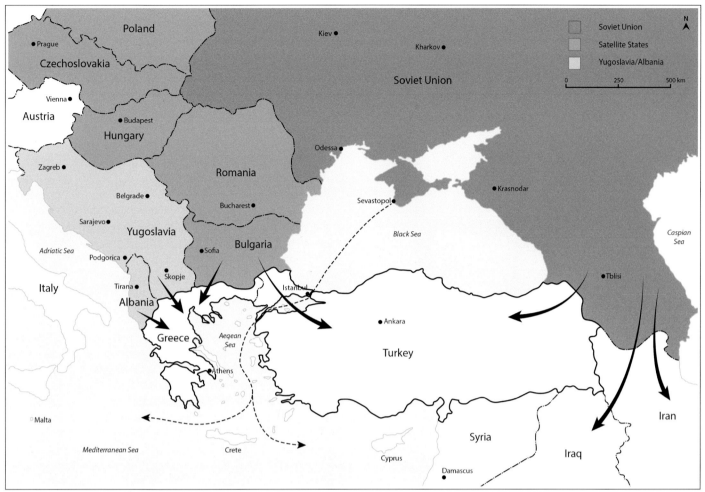

The strategic importance of Greece and Turkey. (George Anderson)

By the end of November, the agreement was finalised and on 2 December 1946, was signed by US Secretary of State James Byrne and British Foreign Secretary Ernest Bevin. As 1947 arrived, a huge swathe of Germany from the North Sea down to the Swiss/Austrian border was under unified economic control and the Bizone (also referred to as Bi-Zone or Bizonia) came into being. At all times the other two occupying powers were kept in the loop, with the door left open in case they wanted to join the British and Americans.[18]

It was a unique organisation founded in very unusual circumstance, so it was inevitable that it would suffer teething problems, which were largely ironed out over the next few months, resulting in a robust structure with many powers devolved to the Länder, including for the first time, creating laws which would directly impact on their people.

President Truman was watching events in Europe with increasing concern. Whilst he may not have agreed with it, he could understand Stalin holding on to countries overrun by the Red Army during the war, but once Stalin began to interfere with countries *outside* the immediate Soviet sphere of influence, it rang serious warning bells in Washington.

In February 1947, the British government informed Washington that it could no longer afford to provide direct financial support to the Greek government and all aid would stop at the end of March. This would not have come as a total surprise, as Great Britain was close to bankruptcy, having mortgaged itself to the hilt to fund the Second World War, but it had serious implications for the stability of the region. The British government had provided financial support to the Greek government during and after the Second World War, recognising its strategic importance: Greece was perfectly positioned

to control the eastern Mediterranean, including access to the Black Sea, the Suez Canal and onwards to the oilfields of the Middle East.

Post-war Great Britain was in a precarious financial situation. It was struggling to rebuild the country, feed its people, meet its debt obligations, fund its occupation of Germany, and maintain its overseas territories. The situation was exacerbated by Truman's abrupt and unexpected termination of the Lend-Lease Program immediately after VJ Day. Great Britain was clearly in no position to continue financing another nation's recovery, so on 21 February 1947, it had no choice but to announce it was withdrawing aid to Greece.

Greece had been gripped by civil war since the end of the Second World War and a communist-led insurgency was fighting Greek government forces. This messy civil war would prove to be very significant as it was the first real proxy battle of the Cold War. The Americans were convinced that Stalin was directly supporting the insurgents, although in reality, he had decided to not intervene, even ordering Yugoslav communist leader Marshall Tito to refrain as well. This may have been a ruse, as he seemed perfectly happy to let Greece's communist neighbours Bulgaria and Albania provide logistical support to the Greek communists.

Truman feared that if Greece was fall to communism, then Turkey would follow. Turkey had remained resolutely neutral during the war and had courted the British, Soviets, the Americans as well as the Nazis. Churchill's offers of British aid, with a view to bringing Turkey into the war on the side of the Allies, were initially rebuffed, although they did end up accepting British support, while managing to stay neutral. By accepting British finance and materiel plus US Lend-Lease Aid in 1945, they inevitably aligned themselves more to the West. As the Cold War developed, a weak government in Ankara faced

General Lucius D. Clay, US Army. (Truman Library)

Soviet pressure to grant base and transit rights through the strategic Dardanelles and Bosphorus Straits, which would have allowed the Soviet Black Sea Fleet to roam freely in the Mediterranean. Turkey was particularly vulnerable to Soviet aggression; from the west via Bulgaria and the Balkans, all along its northern coastline with the Black Sea and in the east from Georgia and Armenia, both then parts of the Soviet Union.

The withdrawal of British aid alongside Soviet aggression threatened to upset the region's balance and Truman was worried that if both Greece and Turkey were to fall to communism, then Stalin's influence was also likely to head south to Iran, across the Middle East and possibly as far east as India. This was what would become known during Eisenhower's Presidency as the Domino Theory, which became a key influence in American Foreign Policy during the early years of the Cold War. The situation also introduced the concept of 'Oil Diplomacy' – Stalin already controlled rich oil fields in the south of the Soviet Union, but if he was to move down into Iran, Iraq and the Arabian Peninsula or west to Turkey and Southern Europe, he could destabilise the whole region and end up holding the world to ransom.

Truman was not prepared to let this happen, and in the first set-piece foreign policy announcement of the new Cold War, he appeared before a joint session of Congress on 12 March 1947 and announced how he planned to contain Soviet expansionism with $400,000,000 (at 1947 value) in military and economic aid for Greece and Turkey. It was a powerful speech, designed to shock both Congress and the American people into action.

> … it must be the policy of the United States to support free peoples who are resisting attempted subjugation by armed minorities or by outside pressures…. The free peoples of the world look to us for support in maintaining their freedoms…. If we falter in our leadership, we may endanger the peace of the world -- and we shall surely endanger the welfare of our own nation.[19]

The policy announced in the speech became known as the Truman Doctrine. This new policy heralded the US taking on the role as 'defender of the free world', which it retains to this day. It also recognised for the first time that US *national* security depended on more than just the *physical* security of US territory.

The speech established that the US would provide political, military and economic assistance to all democratic nations under threat from authoritarian forces, putting Stalin on notice that the US would intervene if he stepped out of line. This applied to Western Europe as well, although it was unclear how it applied to Occupied Germany and the strange situation in West Berlin. Congress approved the bill in May 1947, signalling a step change in US foreign policy using aid as the primary tool. Initially, the aid was focussed on food and raw materials, but once the Marshall Plan closed in 1951, the US government shifted their emphasis to military aid; hardware, investment in overseas bases, local armament factories and sharing the latest technological developments.

With the West beginning to wake up to the threat posed by communism, Stalin realised that he needed to play a waiting game with Germany, hoping that the Western powers could be driven out of Berlin and that a pro-Soviet united Germany may still be possible. So, in March 1947, he told Ulbricht and Grotewohl to slow their all-out drive towards communism in the Soviet Zone and see how the situation developed. By that stage, he had thrown a wide net over eastern Germany – he could afford to wait.

In stark contrast to inter-Allied cooperation seen with the Bizone, the cracks in the ACC were beginning to show, and it was about to get much worse. General Lucius D. Clay became the US Military Governor of Germany on 15 March 1947 and quickly put the cat amongst the pigeons by proposing a separate currency for the Bizone.[20] The old Reichsmarks were causing chaos in the currency markets, driving rampant inflation. The Soviets reacted very badly to Clay's proposal, believing that it would inextricably tie the zones to the West, but eventually agreed that a transition to a new Deutschmark was the only practical way of stabilising the currency markets. However, this step forward soon descended into farce as the parties could not agree where this new currency would be printed. The centre of the historical print industry in Germany lay in Soviet territory, but the Americans did not believe that the Soviets could be trusted. The same East German presses had produced huge amounts of almost perfectly forged British £5 notes during the war and had also printed masses of occupation currency with scant regard for monetary inflation. Combined with the arguments over reparations, the currency debate continued throughout 1947 with the split between the Soviets and her erstwhile allies deepening.

On 20 March 1948, the Soviets withdrew from the Allied Control Council altogether in protest at the work going on in the western zones to create a West German Republic and the ACC effectively ceased to exist. On 16 June 1948, the Soviets also walked out of the Berlin Kommandatura, bringing quadripartite control over Germany to an end.[21] West Berlin's status as a capitalist island in a sea of communism became all the more real.

The Marshall Plan

US Secretary of State, General George C. Marshall was convinced that the future of Europe lay with Germany. He knew that the sooner the Germans became self-sufficient and master of their own destinies, the sooner they would share in the fruits of that recovery and the quicker stability and long-lasting peace would be achieved. However, post-war Occupied Germany was slowly starving and if the situation was not resolved, the ensuing disaster would play right into Stalin's hands. This was exactly the kind of political tinderbox that the Potsdam Conference had tried so hard to avoid.

After six years of war, much of Europe's food production and distribution infrastructure had been destroyed and the economic system around it was grinding to a halt. The introduction of the new

Bizone, merging the British and American economic areas, would eventually improve things, but it was going to take more than an administrative fix to feed their zones. In the meantime, the German population slowly began to starve. As their daily calorie intake dropped below subsistence level, workers began to use up the fat reserves in their bodies which led to muscle wastage, malnutrition and exhaustion, all having a negative impact on health and productivity, both exacerbating the crisis. To add insult to injury, the winter of 1946-47 was particularly harsh, adding much to the population's hardship.

Great Britain was in no real position to help feed the German population in the British Zone. The country had begun to rebuild after the war but was struggling to feed itself and did not even have enough coal to keep the country's lights on.[22] The French also had a country

New American farm machinery being tested in France. (US National Archives via George Marshall Foundation)

to rebuild, but they were in relatively better shape thanks to the rich farmland and industry they had inherited. The problem was, they were not being very cooperative. They deeply resented not being invited to the top table at Potsdam and regularly blocked any attempt for inter-zonal cooperation. The Soviets faced the most devastation during the war, but their zone contained vast swathes of rich agricultural land. The Potsdam agreement allowed for the exchange of Western industrial capital for food and commodities from the Soviet Zone, but with so many mouths to feed, such a reciprocal arrangement was very slow in coming.

The answer was in the financial and industrial might of the United States of America. During the two years since the end of the war, US aid was piecemeal and country specific, including a $3.75 billion loan to Great Britain in 1946, which yielded limited results.[23] Marshall decided that the situation needed a more systematic intervention in order to avoid a re-run of the inter-war depression that fuelled the rise of the Nazis, and also to help the post-war independent states show that they could stand on their own, reducing the opportunities for communism to take hold. He also hoped that Europe would one day become a big market for US goods and also recognised that it paid to have stable prosperous friendly countries in the front line of the new Cold War. He tasked George Kennan, Director of the Policy Planning Staff (known as the S/P) at the State Department with working out 'what could be done to promote world recovery'.

The result of Kennan's team's efforts was announced by Marshall in a relatively low-key speech at Harvard University on 5 June 1947. He stated his objective as 'breaking the vicious circle' of economic decline in the region, and his 'policy [was] directed not against any country or doctrine but against hunger, poverty, desperation and chaos'. He pointedly made no specific mention of communism or Moscow directly, but made it pretty clear that any 'governments, political parties or groups which seek to perpetuate human misery in order to profit there from politically or otherwise will encounter the opposition of the United States.'[24]

The programme was offered widely around post-war Europe, including the Soviet Union and other East European countries but came with conditions. Potential recipients were left in no doubt that participating in the Marshall Plan was akin to joining a private members club – members were expected to behave in a certain way: '… the revival of a working economy in the world so as to permit the emergence of political and social conditions in which free institutions can exist.' The British and French shared similar views and were already broadly in tune with the Americans. For the Soviets, however, it was going to be a big ask; they considered it an extension of the Truman Doctrine, as thinly veiled US economic imperialism or 'Dollar diplomacy' and yet another US attempt at 'capitalist encirclement'. They also fundamentally objected to Germany receiving US aid, not sharing Marshall's optimism for a free and prosperous Europe and seeing a resurgent Germany as a genuine threat.

Whilst being very receptive to Marshall's ideas, the European nations found themselves in a rather curious situation; the speech was deliberately vague but had dangled a massive carrot in front of them with very little official guidance as to how to take up the offer. While publicly insisting that the European countries work together to put a proposal to the US, Marshall's diplomats were working feverishly in the shadows to ensure the discussions succeeded. After some diplomatic wrangling, a meeting was organised in Paris on 26 June 1947 between British Foreign Secretary Ernest Bevin, his French counterpart Georges Bidault, and Soviet Foreign Minister Vyacheslav M. Molotov. Before meeting his counterparts, Molotov felt he was in a strong position – his economists had argued that the US desperately needed the trade the plan would bring to avoid plunging into depression, and therefore the Soviets should be able to dictate their own terms and shape the plan to suit Soviet interests.

Marshall Plan-financed tractors arrive in France. (US National Archives via George Marshall Foundation)

this European cooperation around the Marshall Plan (and the earlier Truman Doctrine) as the first step in an anti-Soviet alliance.

With the Soviets out of the way, Bevin and Bidault widened the discussion to include a further 22 European countries who were invited to a conference in Paris on the 12 July 1947. Eastern European countries that had become wrapped into Stalin's new empire found themselves in a tricky situation. Poland and Czechoslovakia in particular, initially expressed an interest in participating in the negotiations, but Moscow quickly slammed the door on their involvement, threatening the previously independent states of Eastern Europe with grievous consequences if they continued. In the end, 16 countries attended and joined negotiations to pull together a proposal for Washington.

On 19 December 1947, Truman submitted 'A plan for US aid to European Recovery' to Congress. Thanks to considerable bipartisan support, the European Recovery Program passed through relatively smoothly and was written into US Law as the Foreign Assistance Act (a.k.a. the European Cooperation Act) on 3 April 1948. The act pledged around $14 billion of aid between 16 European states over the next 4 years. West Germany would become the 17th recipient in 1949. The money began to flow immediately, and almost $6 billion had been 'spent' by the end of June 1949, with two thirds of the procurement coming from the USA. 31 percent was in the form of raw materials, 36 percent in food, feed and fertiliser, 16 percent in fuel and 14 percent in vehicles and machinery.

However, from the very offset, France and Great Britain challenged the Soviet position, and on 2 July 1947, when it became clear that the British and French were refusing to kowtow to Soviet bullying, Molotov and his 100 strong delegation walked out of the talks, never to return, accusing the US of 'economic imperialism' and a 'hostile capitalist encirclement'. Succumbing to his own Soviet paranoia, he viewed

The impact of this investment was seen quickly, with production levels soon approaching pre-war levels in several of the key European markets. Coal, steel, cement, vehicle and chemical production levels were all up, and agricultural yields grew. Even the economies of the European's overseas dependencies benefited.

By the time the plan had run its course, a total of $13,325,800,000 had been channelled via the Organisation for European Economic Cooperation (OEEC), with around three quarters going to just five recipient states.[25]

The amount of aid received depended on how much a nation had supported the Allied cause during the war and its post-war strategic significance. As a result, Italy did well (scoring high for significance, not support), while Sweden did not.[27] By 1950, industrial production across Europe had grown by 45 percent over the levels when the plan started and was 25 percent higher than pre-war levels. When the programme finished in 1952, industrial production was 200 percent of pre-war levels, while agricultural production was 15 percent up on pre-war levels. The European 'Economic Miracle' had become a reality.

The reasons behind Stalin's rejection of the Marshall Plan in early July 1947 were a bit more complex than the conventional narrative of the deepening divide between the former allies. Stalin felt his global

Table 2: European Recovery Program Recipients: April 3, 1948, to June 30, 1952.[26]		
Country	Current US$ millions	Percentage
Austria	677.8	5 %
Belgium/Luxembourg	559.3	4 %
Denmark	273.0	2 %
France	2,713.6	20 %
Greece	706.7	5 %
Iceland	29.3	Negligible
Ireland	147.5	1 %
Italy	1,508.8	11 %
Netherlands	1,083.5	8 %
Norway	255.3	2 %
Portugal	51.2	Negligible
Sweden	107.3	1 %
Turkey	225.1	2 %
United Kingdom	3,189.8	24 %
West Germany	1,390.6	10 %
Regional	407.0	3 %
TOTAL	**13,325.8**	

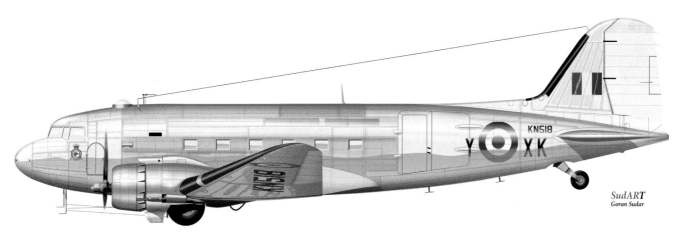

SudART
Goran Sudar

The Douglas Dakota was used extensively by the RAF during the Second World War but by the Berlin Airlift, it was beginning to show its age. Cargo access on the Dakota (and C-47) was only via the side door, which limited its capability. The Dakota was gradually replaced in RAF service by bigger four-engined types such as the Avro York and the Handley Page Hastings. It was also operated by civilian contractors. The aircraft shown is Douglas Dakota Mk. 4 KN518 XK-Y of 46 Squadron RAF. When the aircraft underwent major maintenance, the drab camouflage was removed to save weight, leaving a bare metal finish. (Artwork by Goran Sudar)

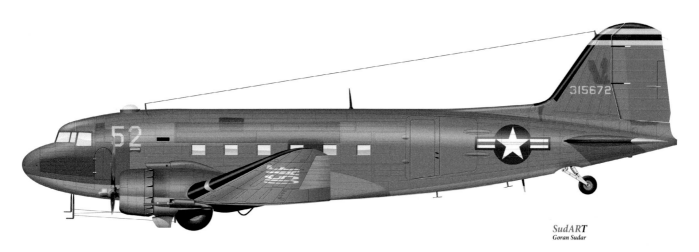

SudART
Goran Sudar

The Douglas C-47 Skytrain was the main aircraft available at the start of the airlift, operated by the USAF as the C-47 and by the RAF as the Dakota. The C-47 was the military version of the civilian DC-3 airliner, designed back in 1934 and had been the mainstay of Allied troop transport during the Second World War, including famously towing gliders and dropping airborne forces on D-Day. It was gradually replaced in USAF service by the bigger and faster four-engined Douglas C-54 Skymaster. The aircraft shown is Douglas C-47 Skytrain 315672 'Yellow 52' USAF. This aircraft can be seen at the bottom of the image on the front cover, unloading at Tempelhof in West Berlin. (Artwork by Goran Sudar)

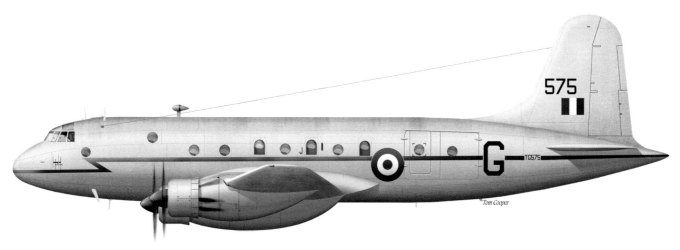

Tom Cooper

Designed to replace the Avro York, the Handley Page Hastings was rushed into service in September 1948 to boost the RAF's airlift capacity, there were a few operational teething problems, but the airlift proved to be its baptism of fire. Like the C-47/Dakota, the Hastings had a side loading-door, which limited its flexibility and one of the key learnings of the airlift was to design transport aircraft with rear or front access to maximise load size and/or accessibility. After an illustrious career, the Hastings was finally retired in 1977. The aircraft shown is Hastings Mk. C1 TG575 'G' of RAF Transport Command, which was written off in a crash at El Adem RAF Station in Libya in 1966. (Artwork by Tom Cooper)

The Short Sunderland was a long-range maritime patrol and anti-submarine flying boat, derived from the pre-war Empire flying boat and operated by RAF Coastal Command. It had two unique characteristics: firstly, aircraft could land on Lake Havel in the British Sector and secondly, it could bring in bulk deliveries of salt. The marinised airframe and high-level control cables meant that it could carry corrosive salt, without risking damage to the airframe. On the return leg of the journey, they brought out civilian passengers and export freight. River operations were based at Finkenwerder on the River Elbe near Hamburg and began in August 1948, continuing until mid-December, when Lake Havel froze. The aircraft shown is Short Sunderland GR Mk. V PP117 '4X-W' of 230 Squadron RAF. The guns were removed to save weight. (Artwork by Goran Sudar)

The four-engined Avro York was reaching the end of its service life but gave Operation Plainfare a much-needed heavy lift capability. Derived from the famous Lancaster bomber, it was roughly equivalent to the US C-54 and first flew in 1942. Around 40 Yorks were used in the operation before being replaced by the Handley Page Hastings. Several Yorks were also used by civilian contractors during the airlift. The aircraft shown is Avro 685 York C.1 MW 271 TB-X of 51 Squadron RAF. The crest just below the pilot's window (and also shown inset) is of RAF Transport Command (A golden griffon in front of a globe). (Artwork by Tom Cooper)

The Bristol Aeroplane Company Freighter (Bristol 170) first flew in December 1945 and was widely used as a military and civilian transport aircraft. During the airlift, it was deployed to ferry heavy equipment over from the UK, such as bulldozers for airfield construction and fire engines, which could be loaded through a wide clam-shell nose. The aircraft were previously being used to ferry cars across the English Channel. The passenger version of the aircraft, the Wayfarer, was also used in the airlift. The aircraft shown is G-AHJC of the Bristol Aeroplane Company, which was on short term lease to Silver City Airways. (Artwork by Luca Canossa)

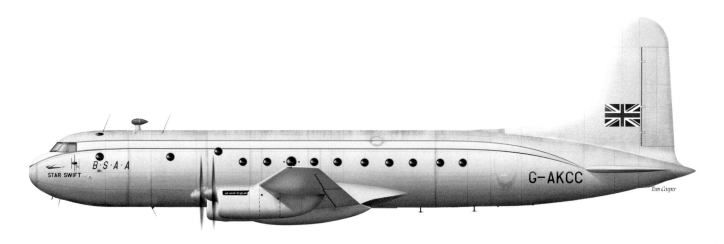

The Avro 689 Tudor Series II was a large four-engine aircraft based on the Avro Lincoln bomber but designed for passenger use. The aircraft was designed by Roy Chadwick, who also designed the Lancaster, York, Lincoln and Vulcan, and first flew in 1946. Chadwick was killed in a take-off accident of the prototype Tudor II, although the accident was caused by a maintenance error, not an inherent design fault. Airflight Ltd and British South American Airways successfully flew Tudors during the airlift, mostly in the tanker configuration. The aircraft shown is Avro Tudor 5 G-AKCC 'Star Swift' of British South American Airways (BSAA). (Artwork by Tom Cooper)

The Avro 691 Lancastrian was the civilian version of the hugely successful Second World War Lancaster bomber. The gun turrets were replaced with aerodynamic fairings and tanks were installed inside the fuselage for bulk transport of liquid fuel. It could transport 1,500 gallons (6,819 litres) of wet fuel, which was the equivalent of about 7 tons. The Lancastrian was operated by Flight Refuelling Ltd and Skyways Ltd. The aircraft shown Avro Lancastrian Mk. CII tanker G-AKMW 'Sky Empire' of Skyways Ltd. (Artwork by Luca Canossa)

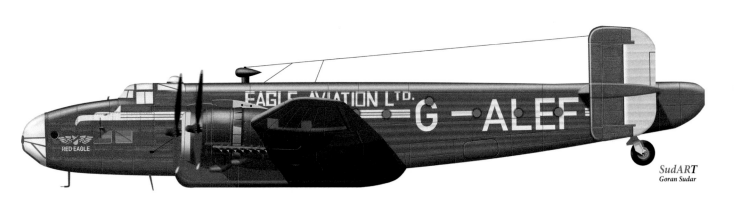

The Handley Page Halton was the civilian version of the Second World War Halifax bomber. Just as with the Lancastrian, the Halton had the gun turrets replaced with aerodynamic fairings. The Halton had a large removable 'pannier' in place of the bomb bay, allowing bulk freight to be carried 'outside' the airframe. This was ideal for the shipment of bulk salt when ice curtailed RAF Short Sunderland river operations. The Halton was named after RAF Halton, the RAF Apprentice training base in Halton, Buckinghamshire and was operated by BAAS, Bond Air Services, Eagle Aviation, Lancashire Aircraft Corporation, Skyflight, Westminster Airways and World Air Freight. The aircraft shown is Handley Page Halton G-ALEF 'Red Eagle' of Eagle Aviation, adding an unusual splash of colour to the airlift. (Artwork by Goran Sudar)

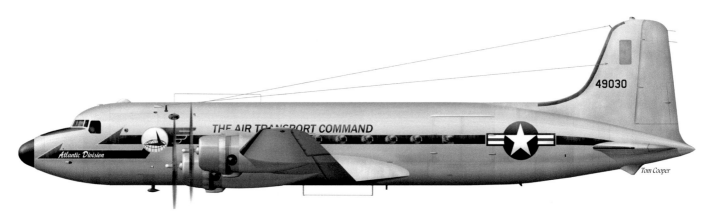

The C-54 Skymaster was the military version of the Douglas DC-4 airliner and replaced the ageing C-47, carrying almost three times its load and cruising around 30mph faster. The C-54s began operating on 1 July 1948 and were responsible for around a third of the total airlift, completely replacing the US C-47 fleet by 1 October 1948. The USAF C-54s were joined by US Navy R5Ds, with the fleet eventually growing to 225 aircraft. The aircraft shown is C-54M 44-9030 (tail number 49030) of the USAF Military Air Transport Service (MATS), Atlantic Division. It was specially converted to carry coal during the airlift and was assigned to 513th Air Transport Group, Rhein Main AB, Germany in January 1949, and then to 316th Troop Carrier Group Heavy, at Celle AB, Germany in April 1949. (Artwork by Tom Cooper)

The Douglas C-74 Globemaster's contribution to the airlift was mostly in ferrying aircraft engines and urgent spares from the US to the huge American airbases in West Germany. It could carry a massive 48,150 lb (21,840 kg) of cargo and had a 3,400-mile range. The aircraft was too heavy to land on PSP, but RAF Gatow in Berlin had a suitable concrete runway, although its arrival disrupted the steady flow of normal airlift traffic. Loading and unloading was made easy by its unusual freight loading elevator, where a section of the rear fuselage big enough to carry a jeep would be lowered on cables. The aircraft shown is 42-65414 (tail number 265414), 'CN-414' of the USAF Military Air Transport Service (MATS), which made around 25 trips to West Berlin over six weeks in August/September 1948, carrying mostly flour and coal. It also carried construction equipment for use in the construction of Tegel Airfield in the French sector. The equipment, including a rock crusher, was too big for even the Globemaster to accommodate, so it was cut into pieces at Rhein-Main, flown to West Berlin aboard the C-74 and welded back together at Tegel. (Artwork by Tom Cooper)

The C-82 was an unusual twin boomed transport aircraft, with a wide rear loading door and high tail assembly, allowing large items to be loaded, such as construction equipment to build extra runways, fire trucks and ambulances. Although it was slow and relatively unsophisticated, its rear access design was echoed (albeit without the twin boom tail) in future transport aircraft designs. The name 'Packet' comes from the 18th century Packet Ships that delivered mail, passengers and freight between Great Britain and her colonies. The aircraft shown is Fairchild C-82A-FA Packet 45-57740 (tail number 557740) 'CQ-740'. It was operated by various units from September 1948 to September 1949 at Wiesbaden AB and then at Rhein-Main AB until October 1949. (Artwork by Tom Cooper)

The US Constabulary was created in July 1946 to concentrate on policing the occupation throughout the whole American Zone, a task normal US infantry was not well suited to. It was created as a highly mobile mechanized elite force using armoured cars, tanks, jeeps, motorcycles and other vehicles outfitted with full radio and signal equipment, plus horse mounted troops for riot control. They wore a distinctive uniform and were known as the 'Circle C Cowboys' after their highly polished helmets with a blue stripe sandwiched between two bright yellow stripes going around the helmet, with the Constabulary insignia, a big 'C' in a circle on the front. The Germans called them the 'Lightning Police' after the lightning bolt on their shoulder flash. The trooper shown is armed with a M1911 semi-automatic .45 calibre pistol. Troopers also carried M1 Garand rifles and M3 sub-machine guns.

The *Deutsche Volkspolizei* (German People's Police or DVP) evolved from the communist German auxiliary police force, which had been established in the Soviet Zone soon after VE Day. The *Volkspolizei* (or VP), known colloquially as VoPos, became an integral part of the highly militarised East German police state. The Vopo shown is a Wachtmeister, roughly equivalent to a Feldwebel or Sergeant. He is wearing the distinctive Tschako helmet, made of pressed fibre, with a scaled metal chin strap. The helmet badge features the national emblem of the DDR: a hammer and compass, surrounded by a ring of rye. He holds a Sturmgewehr (StG) 44 assault rifle (known locally as the MPi.44). Designed during the Second World War by Hugo Schmeisser, it fired a 7.92×33mm Kurz cartridge, and was considered the world's first proper assault rifle. The MPi.44 was replaced by the Soviet PPSh-41 sub-machine gun in Vopo service by the early 1960s. (Artwork by Anderson Subtil)

The pilots were the unsung heroes of the Berlin Airlift, undertaking two, three and sometimes four missions a day, requiring precision flying and to-the-minute accuracy as part of a well-oiled machine. They also had to endure very basic facilities back at base. The officer shown is a Flight Lieutenant from 206 Squadron, 46 (Transport) Group, RAF Transport Command, flying the Avro York C1 from RAF Wunstorf in West Germany to RAF Gatow in West Berlin. He is wearing standard RAF overalls, flying boots and side cap. The badge on his left breast pocket, shown in detail inset, is of RAF Transport Command. (Artwork by Anderson Subtil)

Wherever British troops were stationed, they would be accompanied by the Corps of Royal Military Police, tasked with maintaining law and order within the British Forces community. Known as the RMP or 'Redcaps' (because of the bright red covers on their caps), they worked alongside the British Civil Authorities across the British Zone. In Berlin, the RMP had the additional role of liaising with their counterparts in the American, French and Soviet sectors. 247 (Berlin) Provost Company, 2 Regiment, Royal Military Police were stationed in the city and maintained a very high profile, ensuring that Great Britain's Four-Power rights were maintained. The soldier shown is a Lance Corporal and is carrying a service revolver (either the Enfield No. 2 or Webley Mk V1) attached to a lanyard. Military Policemen wore distinctive high visibility white blancoed webbing. The badge shown is of the Berlin Brigade. (Artwork by Anderson Subtil)

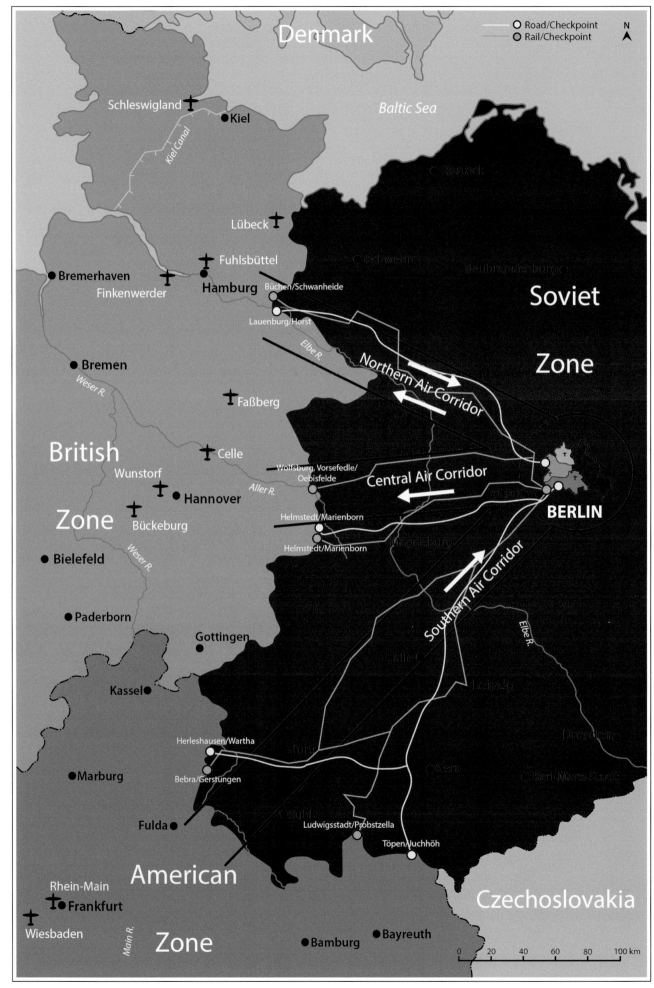

The British, American and Soviet zones of Germany and the air, road and rail corridors to Berlin. (Map by George Anderson)

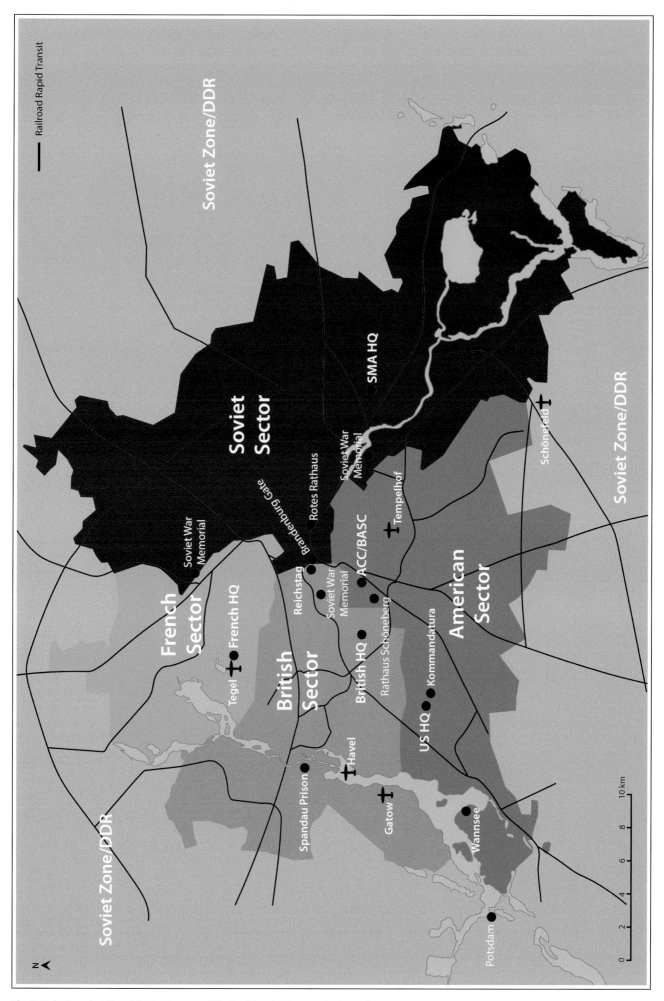

The British, French, US and Soviet Sectors of Berlin. (Map by George Anderson)

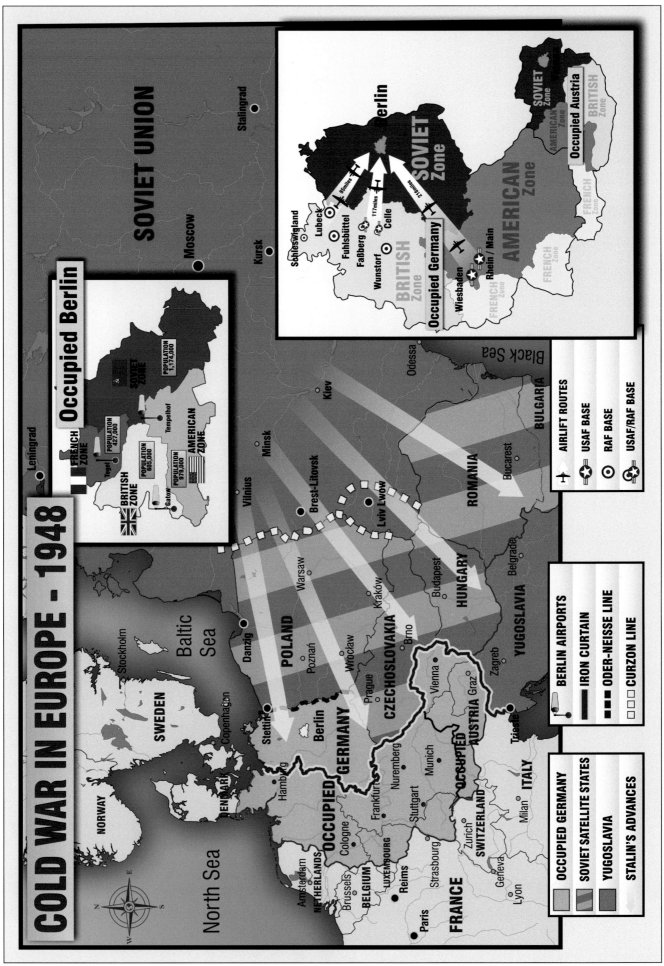

COLD WAR IN EUROPE – 1948

Occupied Berlin

SOVIET UNION

Stalingrad

Moscow

Kursk

FRENCH ZONE

SOVIET ZONE

POPULATION 1,174,000

Tempelhof

Leningrad

AMERICAN ZONE

POPULATION 427,000

Tegel

POPULATION 605,000

POPULATION 979,000

BRITISH ZONE

Gatow

Occupied Germany

Berlin

SOVIET Zone

Schleswigland

Lubeck

Fuhlsbüttel

Faßberg

35 miles

21 miles

117 miles

Celle

Wunstorf

Rhein / Main

Wiesbaden

BRITISH Zone

AMERICAN Zone

FRENCH Zone

FRENCH Zone

SOVIET Zone

AMERICAN Zone

BRITISH Zone

Occupied Austria

Black Sea

Odessa

Kiev

BULGARIA

ROMANIA

Bucarest

Minsk

Vilnius

Brest-Litovsk

Lviv Lwów

HUNGARY

Budapest

Belgrade

YUGOSLAVIA

Zagreb

Warsaw

Kraków

Danzig

Poznań

Wrocław

Prague

Brno

Baltic Sea

Stockholm

SWEDEN

POLAND

CZECHOSLOVAKIA

Vienna

AUSTRIA Graz

Trieste

Stettin

Berlin

OCCUPIED GERMANY

Nuremberg

Munich

OCCUPIED SWITZERLAND

Zurich

Geneva

Milan

ITALY

Copenhagen

DENMARK

Hamburg

Frankfurt

Stuttgart

Strasbourg

Cologne

NORWAY

North Sea

Amsterdam

NETHERLANDS

BELGIUM

Brussels

LUXEMBOURG

Reims

Paris

FRANCE

Lyon

Geneva

AIRLIFT ROUTES
USAF BASE
RAF BASE
USAF/RAF BASE

BERLIN AIRPORTS
IRON CURTAIN
ODER–NEISSE LINE
CURZON LINE

OCCUPIED GERMANY
SOVIET SATELLITE STATES
YUGOSLAVIA
STALIN'S ADVANCES

In the years following the Second World War, Europe became the frontline in the new 'Cold War' as Stalin 'built' his Iron Curtain and tried to force his former allies from Berlin by blockading the city. The West responded with the Berlin Airlift, saving West Berlin's population from starvation. (Map by Anderson Subtil)

standing to be weak in the early years of the Cold War, and he was much more focussed on shoring up his 'Ring of Steel' than he was with any plans for aggressive westward expansion. Until he rebuilt his country and acquired nuclear parity with the Americans (which he would not do until August 1949 at the earliest), Stalin felt especially vulnerable and this US initiative backed him dangerously into a corner. In addition, the continued absence of a satisfactory negotiated settlement over Germany was just as unsettling for the Soviet leader; he was banking on getting significant war reparations towards Soviet reconstruction and genuinely was worried that Germany could rise again to be a threat to the Motherland, so as far as he was concerned, any inclusion of negotiation on the status of Germany was firmly off the table.

Whilst the primary objective of the Marshall Plan was defensive, that is, to help Europe's economies recover and be in a stronger position to counter future Soviet aggression, it was also deliberately provocative, openly enticing Eastern European nations away from their Moscow masters. Stalin had fought hard for this territory, expending the blood of many thousands of his troops and did not want to see it eroded, thus exposing chinks in his defensive protection. He was also suspicious of the West's designs on Eastern Europe's rich supply of raw materials. He viewed all of it, somewhat understandably, as a genuine threat to his national security and helped fuel his already acute paranoia.

The Americans knew that Stalin was never going to agree to the conditions they were stipulating, but the very act of making the offer gave the US the moral high ground. Propaganda from both sides blamed each other for failure to agree on terms for the Soviets to accept the plan; the Americans said it was yet another indication that the Soviet Union intended to impose communist doctrine across Europe (which at the time actually was not the case), while the Soviets rejected US economic imperialism and unwarranted meddling in their internal affairs. From the Soviet perspective, their rejection of the plan could be seen as natural opposition to being forced to integrate a fervently non-capitalist state into an overt capitalist system, and why should they help to keep America out of a post-war depression? Further negotiations would therefore be futile. Stalin also knew that accepting US money would open his very closed society up to external scrutiny and he had cupboards and cupboards full of skeletons that he would rather remain hidden.[28]

Under these circumstances, it is easy to see why Stalin's reaction to the US's offer of aid was so extreme – Stalin fought back with bluster and bravado, trying to compensate for his perceived position of weakness. His crude and aggressive moves over Iran, Turkey and Berlin in the immediate post-war years can be understood as natural responses to Western threats against Soviet sovereignty just as much as Soviet attempts at territorial expansion or loud sabre-rattling to camouflage and compensate for a position of relative weakness.

Moscow's rejection of the Marshall Plan can also be viewed as one element of the 'Molotov plan'; a deliberate strategy to further the aims of the Soviet Union that had been in place since the end of the Second World War. This 'plan' included the removal of much of the surviving industrial capital and infrastructure from the areas of Nazi Germany that the Soviets had occupied, either as official reparations or simply as state-sponsored looting on a massive scale. Moscow also engineered a programme of Sovietisation and a series of political 'coups' in the satellite states that bordered the Soviet Union to ensure their governments would yield to Moscow's authority.[29]

Although Moscow yielded a big 'stick', Stalin recognised that some 'carrot' was needed to give his satellite states a degree of cohesion. Representatives from the governments of these states met in Poland from 22 to 27 September 1947 to create the Cominform, the Communist Information Bureau. The Cominform was a partial revival of the Comintern (the Communist International), which Stalin had disbanded in 1943. While Cominform's scope was more European and less revolutionary, it still focussed on building a common strategy across European Communist parties under the control of the Soviet Union against their common enemy – American imperialism.

Cominform's role was initially to mobilise resistance to the Marshall Plan across Europe, trying to stop the formation of an anti-communist block amongst Marshall Plan recipients. European communists, in particular the French and Italians, were told to do their best to obstruct the take up of the Marshall Plan in their respective countries through widespread industrial action. Andrei Zhdanov, Stalin's chief ideologue, used the inaugural meeting of the Cominform to confirm the view (as previously identified by Kennan in his 'Long Telegram') that the world was irreconcilably split into two opposing camps; an 'imperialist and anti-democratic' camp led by the United States and an 'anti-imperialist and democratic' camp led by the Soviet Union. This concept, originally proposed by Marx and as referenced by Kennan, became known as the Zhdanov Doctrine, which, along with the Marshall Plan, caused Moscow's attitude to harden and widened the divide between East and West.

The American aid programmes coincided with the build-up of US and British troops in Europe, particularly in Germany, which had the bonus effect of pumping millions of dollars into host nation's economies; an indirect way of boosting the aid programmes and further cementing the Western Alliance. Marshall's original goal of reducing the US military commitment in Europe would not be fulfilled as the dangerous realities of the new Cold War overtook the previous thinking.

The Marshall Plan was far from perfect and had many critics, but the aid had the effect of saving the western zones of Germany from collapse at a critical time and demonstrating the resolve of the growing Western Alliance. This resolve was about to be severely tested.

4

AN ISLAND CITY: THE BERLIN BLOCKADE AND AIRLIFT

The city of Berlin was located 100 miles (160km) inside the Soviet Zone. When the European Advisory Commission (EAC) was working out the details of how to administer Germany and Berlin through the three (and subsequently four) Zones of Occupation, the key issue of access for the Western Allies to West Berlin was left unresolved. As a point of principle, the US and British (and latterly the French) did not want to accept *specific* routes, as that would concede the denial of passage of *all* routes to the city, a situation that the Allies could not accept. They were also convinced that the division of Germany was only a temporary arrangement and an acceptable permanent

Ernst Reuter, Mayor of West Berlin , more normally seen wearing a black beret. (US Army Military History Institute)

peace treaty was only months away. They also believed that the spirit of wartime inter-Allied cooperation would continue in the peace. This intransigence, wishful-thinking and naivety would have serious consequences for the city in a relatively short period of time.

In order to get things moving after the war ended, the Western Allies accepted a temporary arrangement which identified a corridor across Soviet territory to the Western sectors of the city comprising a road, rail and air route. They subsequently agreed on limited canal/waterway access. The Allies reserved the right to re-negotiate this at the ACC, but the Soviet veto meant that permanent access arrangements could be put off indefinitely, creating a very dangerous precedent. The Soviets insisted that the Western Powers supplied their own sectors with food, fuel and consumer goods and with no reserves, natural resources or food production facilities to speak of everything the city needed, from fuel to soap had to imported along these corridors. This irritating resupply arrangement had the unexpected advantage of establishing logistics routes and hubs in the Western Zones of Occupation, which would prove rather useful in years to come.

Thanks to its unique situation, Berlin was always going to be a weak spot for the West, and Stalin knew he would have to pile on the pressure if he wanted them to abandon their tenuous grip on the city. He began a campaign of mischief and disruption and the Western Allies soon began to understand that the Soviets could disrupt life in the city any time they wanted. The SMA started small, spreading rumours, such as the Allies were about to pull out of the city and other destabilising dis-information. As they controlled the media, this propaganda was allowed to spread unchallenged. They regularly began to disrupt the transport system, demanding inspections of papers and freight, irritating the locals who were just trying to get on with their daily lives. They also began disrupting city politics, such as vetoing the appointment of Ernst Reuter, the newly elected (and ex-communist) Mayor of the city in June 1947.

These stunts soon took on a sinister tone; squads of heavily armed troops were seen roaming around the streets and Berliners seen carrying Western newspapers in the Soviet sector were likely

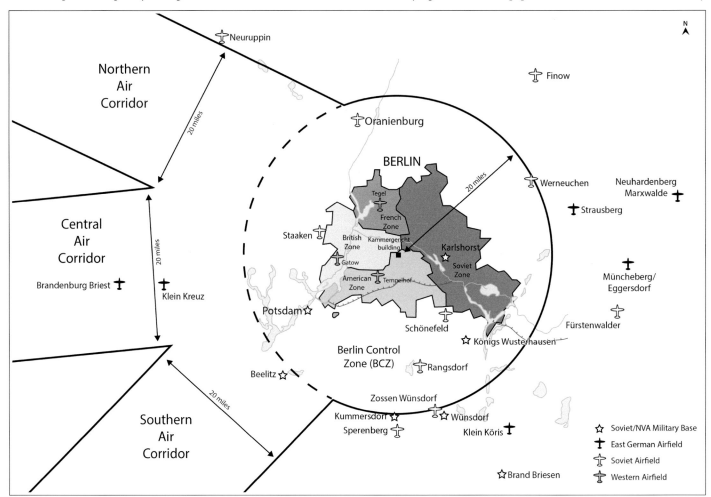

Berlin Airspace, with Berlin Control Zone, end of Air Corridors and Airfields. (George Anderson)

to be arrested. In an excuse that would be regularly repeated by East Germany's leaders, the SMA complained of 'bandits' and 'criminal elements' entering their sector, which in their eyes was justification for the disruption. All this was designed to undermine the confidence of the West Berliners and make them worry about the sort of reprisals they could expect from the Soviets if the Allies *did* abandon the city.

Life in Berlin was tough, with constant hunger, fuel shortages, a thriving black market and gangs of orphaned children roaming the city. Enterprising British and American troops stationed in the city could become very wealthy by trading on this black market. However, the citizens of Berlin were a resilient bunch, having survived the war itself, the destruction of the Third Reich on their very doorstep and the hordes of marauding Red Army troops invading their city. A key factor that helped Berliners through these hardships was the *Berliner Schnauz*, literally Berliner 'Snout'; a healthy cynical 'in your face' attitude, similar to that of the Cockneys who lived through the Blitz in London's East End or New Yorkers from the Bronx or Brooklyn. Their resilience was about to be tested yet again.

The Corridors

On 30 November 1945, the ACC established the 'Berlin Control Zone' (BCZ), 10,000 ft (3,048m) high controlled airspace across a 20-mile (32km) radius from the old Kammergericht (Supreme Court) building in the district of Schönberg. The Control Zone would be managed by the Four-Power Allied Air Security Headquarters, based in the building. The agreement also established three air corridors into the city, each terminating in the Berlin Control Zone. Each corridor was 20 miles wide and permitted traffic up to 10,000ft. The northern route was from the direction of Hamburg flying across 95 miles (153km) of Soviet territory in a south-easterly direction, servicing RAF Gatow in the British sector. Gatow was an ex-Luftwaffe training base and also provided the destination for the central corridor, flying eastwards from the direction of Bückeburg (Hannover) over 117 miles (188km) of the Soviet Zone. The longest route came from the direction of Frankfurt in the south, flying in a north-easterly direction over the Taunus mountains for 216 miles (347km) and landing at Tempelhof, Berlin's pre-war civilian airport, now located in the US sector. A further airstrip would be built at Tegel in the French sector, which opened in December 1948 and was served by both the northern and central corridors. In theory, all British, French and American aircraft had freedom of passage along these corridors and in the Berlin Control Zone, without having to notify the Soviets in advance and as long as they stayed clear of any Soviet airfields. Conditions were fairly basic at these bases, with no radio or navigational aids for the pilots and in some cases, even without adequate runways.

By early 1948, the Soviet campaign of disruption escalated, and they began stopping trains, demanding to inspect the papers of any civilian passengers. Military personnel were exempt from this inspection but suffered the delays all the same, with officious Soviets stopping freight trains and inspecting every piece of freight. If the officials on the train kicked up a fuss, their train would be shunted into a siding and left for hours. Drivers risking the autobahn corridor were also inconvenienced by roadblocks to inspect papers and random closures for 'repairs'. The Soviets began accusing the Western Allies of aiding and abetting the illegal flow of goods and people into the city and, in language that would become all too familiar, announced that action would have to be taken to 'protect' the inhabitants of the city against 'subversive and terrorist elements'.

The Soviets steadily began to tighten their vice-like hold over the city and make life really intolerable for the inhabitants of the western sectors and their defenders. In April 1948, they began demanding document and baggage checks for *all* Western nationals crossing the Soviet Zone en route to Berlin, *including* military personnel and military freight trains. The Allies were not prepared to accept that, so they suspended all military rail traffic, choosing to resupply their garrisons by air instead. Clay organised a mini airlift which shipped 327 tons of cargo on 33 flights between the 1 and 12 April 1948, which became known as the 'Little Lift' or the 'Baby Blockade'. On the 12 April, the Soviets stopped demanding the inspections and normal traffic resumed, although the US continued daily resupply flights shipping people and equipment back and forth. This mini blockade highlighted the vulnerability of their troops stationed in the city and the three Allied powers began planning how to mitigate any further disruption. They began increasing stockpiles of staple goods and evacuating unnecessary personnel. For example, they bumped up coal shipments from 1,500 tons in March to 12,000 tons in April and 10,000 in May. They also began to position transport resources in the western zones of Germany, just in case. The British plan to resupply their garrison (and also evacuate the families of British servicemen) was called Operation Knicker and was completed in early June. It called for two Dakota (C-47) squadrons comprising 16 aircraft, flying 65 tons a day from bases in Britain over to Berlin. However, in London and Washington, the powers-that-be genuinely did not believe the Soviets would try anything as serious as an all-out blockade.

The Soviets then began disrupting canal traffic around the city and outgoing mail as well. Soon the northern and southern rail routes were shut down, with all rail traffic having to go via Helmstedt on the central corridor, which caused major disruption. Allied protests fell on deaf ears as the inter-Allied forum, the ACC had collapsed, and they had no legal agreement to fall back on anyway.

Back in London, Paris and Washington, politicians expressed their outrage and the Soviets' behaviour while their planners and logisticians rapidly began to look at ways to supply the German public and their defenders across the British, French and American sectors. General Lucius Clay, the US Military Governor and head of US forces in Europe, recommended standing up to the Soviet intransigence and deliver a show of force. He predicted his own version of the 'Domino Effect', some years before Eisenhower coined the phrase – lose Berlin and you lose Germany to communism, lose Germany and you lose Europe, lose Europe …. To counter the latest Soviet obstructions, he proposed sending an armoured column by road to protect the truck convoy delivering supplies. His boss, General Omar Bradley, the US Army Chief of Staff, however, demurred, recognising that a highway confrontation could easily lead to a 'shooting war' and ordered Clay to 'wait and see'. The Allies did, however, agree to a counter-blockade, stopping steel, chemicals, other raw materials and manufactured goods from entering the Soviet sector and beyond, as well as refusing passage of goods trains transiting the western sectors of Berlin. The sanctions were not going to cause the East Germans and Soviets too much trouble in the short term, but they showed the communists that the Allies were not going to take the Soviet aggression lying down.

The obvious solution was to use the air corridors. During the Second World War, the US had successfully executed a massive airlift from India across the 'Hump' of the Himalayas to China in support of the Chinese troops fighting the Japanese in south China and Burma and the British had air-dropped supplies to the starving Dutch at the end of the Second World War, although Goering spectacularly failed in his promised air resupply at Stalingrad. The Allied European air strength was seriously depleted by the post-war draw-down and were therefore dangerously outnumbered by the Soviets, who still remained on a war-footing. Initial air tests using Second World War surplus Douglas C-47s from the Rhein-Main US air base near Frankfurt proved the

German currency stamped B for Berlin. (US Army Military History Institute)

delivered to the old Reichsbank building in Frankfurt/Main.[3] The authorities also wanted to get the potentially unpopular introduction out of the way well before the planned creation of a new West German government. The introduction was covered by the 'First Law on Currency Reform' which came in to force on Sunday 20 June 1948, invalidating the old Reichsmark and replacing it with the Deutsche Mark, which was split into 100 Deutsche Pfennig. A Sunday was chosen to allow for a degree of disruption that would hopefully be resolved by the start of business on Monday. The law laid down detailed arrangements for the exchange of currency and measures to stop a) people losing out and b) speculators taking advantage of the change.[4]

The initial issue of D-Marks *did not* include the Western sectors of Berlin, which the British, Americans and French considered to still be under Four-Power rule. They were to continue using the old Reichsmarks, over-printed with a large 'B', thus avoiding a flood of old currency into the city from the Western zones.

On the day of the announcement, the Western Military Governors wrote to their Soviet counterpart, General Sokolovsky, informing him of the impending change. Sokolovsky's response was brutal, stating that the terms of the Potsdam Declaration which stipulated that Germany be treated as an economic whole had been violated, that the new Western currency would be invalid within the Soviet Zone and 'Greater' Berlin, and possession of it would constitute a criminal offence. He also decided to suspend highway and railway passenger traffic to and from Berlin and reduced freight traffic effective at midnight, supposedly to 'protect' the Soviet Zone from an influx of the old, devalued currency.

On 22 June, the three Western Occupying Powers attempted to discuss the currency reforms with the Soviets, hoping to negotiate a single currency for the whole city. However, as experienced in most quadripartite discussions, the Soviets would not agree to the West's proposals, arguing that *only* they had the right to dictate currency policy for the city of Berlin, seeing as it was located within their Zone of Occupation and also that they no longer recognised the authority of the Kommandatura (the forum they had walked out of a few days earlier on 16 June) as the supreme law-making body for Berlin. In response to the introduction of the D-Mark, on 24 June, the SMA announced that they were creating a new currency for the Soviet Zone, the Ost Mark and so the Allied powers had no option but to extend the currency reforms to the three sectors of West Berlin as well. The Soviet solution for the introduction of the Ost Mark was clearly last-minute – they would attach a coupon to the old Reichsmarks until the new East or Ost Marks were printed.

Both sides had anticipated a scrap over the currency reforms: the Soviets saw them as another opportunity to beat the West up over their rights to West Berlin, and the West had expected some negative reaction to their proposals and had begun to stockpile supplies in the Western

concept, although on 5 April 1948, a British Vickers Viking of British European Airways crashed after colliding with a Soviet fighter, killing all 10 passengers and crew plus the Soviet pilot. On 17 April, three Soviet fighters made aggressive close passes on an American aircraft. Following these two incidents, British or American fighters were made available to escort civilian flights if Soviet activity was reported along the corridors. The planners also began secretly establishing forward supply bases in France and Belgium using USAF personnel in civilian clothing.

Early in June, the situation escalated rapidly. Over in London, the three Western Allies met to discuss the future of Germany; that is, the three zones of Germany that they controlled. On 7 June 1948, they issued a communique announcing the steps they were taking to begin rehabilitating Germany as a State in its own right.[1] This process had begun at the end of 1946, with the British and Americans merging their zones economically to form the Bizone. While the French decided to stay out of this formal arrangement at the time, it still rang warning bells with Stalin in Moscow, who was still hoping to reunify Germany under a Soviet banner. The 7 June communique announced further economic cooperation moving towards the eventual formation of a British/American/French Trizone, and the first steps towards a new provisional West German government.

Stalin took great exception to these efforts towards forming a new German state and ordered an aggressive response from his forces in Berlin. On the 11 June 1948, all railroad freight traffic between the western zones and Berlin were suspended by the Soviets for two days. On the 15 June 1948, they closed the autobahn bridge over the River Elbe 'for repairs', forcing a 90 minute diversion via the ferry.

The final straw for Stalin was the announcement on Friday 18 June at an evening OMGUS press-conference in Frankfurt, the soon-to-be financial centre of West Germany, which announced that a new currency was to be launched for the western zones; the Deutsche Mark or D-Mark.[2] The announcement of the sweeping currency reforms had been kept secret for several reasons; to allow the authorities to amass sufficient stocks of the new bank notes, to avoid currency speculation or black market activity and to avoid retaliatory action from the Soviets. The new currency, packed in 23,000 boxes cryptically marked 'Bird Dog' and weighing 1,035 tons, was secretly

zones. However, the scale of the blockade and the proposed Allied relief operation surprised even the most pessimistic of planners. Fundamentally, both sides recognised that this was a deciding moment in post-war European history, sealing the fate for a divided Germany.

Siege

On the day the new D-Mark was introduced, the blockade began to roll out. The first to go was an American military train, which was halted at Marienborn. The Soviets claimed 'technical difficulties were to blame, which was technically true as they had ripped the track up on their side of the border! On the 23 June, they cut off the supply of electricity from the power station in their sector. By Thursday 24 June, they had suspended all road and barge traffic, cut off the water and electrical supplies and halted all supplies of coal, food and milk. West Berlin was now under siege.

The political reaction in the West took a few days to reach a consensus. They faced a stark choice: they could not let the city starve, but should they admit defeat and abandon the city to the Soviets, or should they bite the bullet and find a way to resupply the city for as long as it was needed? In Washington, some of Truman's advisors and generals advocated the use of military force, while others urged caution, questioning whether Berlin was worth taking a stand over. Clay reiterated his proposal to send an armed convoy along the autobahn responding to aggressive or violent Soviet actions with reciprocal force, while Lieutenant General Curtiss E. LeMay, commander of the US Airforce in Europe (USAFE) said if the convoy met serious resistance, he would attack every Soviet airfield in eastern Germany on the assumption that the Soviets had started World War Three!

Short of an atomic strike, a localised military solution was

'To supply the island of Berlin with the necessities of life by air'. (Albert Grandolini)

C-47 aircraft are parked on the ramp at Rhein-Main Air Base, Frankfurt, Germany. They are being loaded with food and supplies to be flown to Templehof Air Base in Berlin during Operation Vittles. (Truman Library)

Loading apron at RAF Wunstorf with RAF Yorks and a Dakota. (Albert Grandolini)

Tempelhof Airdrome in the American sector of West Berlin before the airlift, July 1946. (Edwin W. Pauley via Truman Library)

An airborne resupply operation would require an unprecedented logistical effort by the Western Powers, with a lengthy and complex supply chain across Europe and operations reverting to something close to a war-footing. All this was based on the assumption that sufficient aircraft and supplies could be made available. It was going to be an enormous challenge.

The story of the Berlin Airlift covers many topics, but the recurring themes are those of a herculean effort against impossible odds, an international operation on an epic scale, innovation in the face of adversity, the professionalism and bravery of thousands of troops, aircrew, ground crew and civilians and the single-minded determination of the Allied governments and the citizens of West Berlin not to be beaten by the Soviets. Their mission statement was straightforward:

To supply the island of Berlin with the necessities of life by air.[6]

The Second World War had been over for three years and although the occupying powers still maintained sizeable army garrisons along with air assets in their zones, these represented a small percentage of the resources available in-theatre at the end of the conflict. The draw-down had sent home millions of troops, disposed of vehicles and aircraft, and closed down bases and other military infrastructure. The role of the occupying forces was very different to the fighting force that beat the Nazis – the British Army of the Rhine (BAOR) and United States Army, Europe (USAREUR) were there primarily to support their respective military governments and police their Zones of Occupation. The air assets under the British Air Forces of Occupation (BAFO) and US Air Force Europe (USAFE) command were primarily fighter-based, tasked with intercepting and shooting down enemy aircraft or supporting ground troops. The strategic bomber and transport functions were much reduced. The number of usable transport aircraft in-theatre was therefore very small, and the infrastructure needed to support large scale transport logistics simply did not exist.

The only transport aircraft in-theatre were used to ferry personnel, mail and equipment from base to base around Europe and also to support army operations. This amounted to only seven or so British C-47s (including the personal VIP transport for the BAFO's senior officer) and around 70 American aircraft from the 60th and 61st Troop Carrier Groups. The 61st had around 25 C-47s at Rhein-Main, which was ideally placed to supply the city along the southern corridor, but the rest were located with the 60th way down south in Bavaria, at Kaufbeuren.[7] Way too small a force to handle the anticipated tonnage.

As well as having limited aircraft, the ground facilities also left a lot to be desired, both in western Germany and in West Berlin. The American fighter base at Rhein-Main had a 6,000ft (1,829 metres)

clearly out of the question given the lack of military resources in-theatre and the overwhelming superiority of Soviet forces in the city and surrounding countryside.[5] Truman recognised the importance of Berlin to the post-war security of Europe and overruled the doubters, ordering an all-out effort to keep the city supplied. In London, the British government confirmed they would defend their right to be in the city and mobilised the resupply effort.

With road, rail and waterway access cut off, the only viable option was using the three air corridors and beginning an airlift to fly supplies into the city from bases located inside the western zones of Germany. Although the Allied powers had plans in place for a limited garrison resupply, they really had not considered the option of supplying a city of 2.2 million people with all their daily needs. General Clay and his British counterpart, General Sir Brian H. Robertson were acutely aware that the western sectors of Berlin were in a very precarious position – they calculated that there were only three or four weeks' worth of food, fuel and other supplies to keep West Berlin going and they made sure their lords and masters were aware of the fact.

runway with a few aircraft hardstands dotted around it but was otherwise known as 'Rhein-Mud' because of the poor ground conditions, while nearby Wiesbaden only had a 5,500ft runway and minimal facilities. The British base at Wunstorf was better equipped, with two concrete runways along with taxiways and aprons for aircraft handling.

The two Berlin airfields fared no better. Aircraft landed on Pierced Steel Planking (PSP), interlinked sheets of pressed steel pierced with a series of holes for drainage, but still took off from grass. Tempelhof in the American sector embodied elegant 1930s air travel but had been badly bombed during the war and was hardly suitable for large scale logistics operations.

Gatow, in the British sector, also had a PSP runway but its concrete runway was still under construction and incomplete when the airlift began. None of the airfields were set up for the handling of bulk shipments. Accommodation for personnel was rudimentary, to say the least, comprising tents, Nissan huts and other temporary wooden buildings, with totally inadequate sanitary facilities.[8]

The Airlift Begins

It was from this inauspicious beginning that the Berlin Airlift began, with the first few aircraft arriving on 21 June. US C-47s flew in supplies for the US garrison from the US base at Rhein-Main to Tempelhof in the American sector. On 24 June, in response to the full Soviet shutdown, the BAFO implemented Operation Knicker to keep the British garrison supplied. Eight Dakotas

USAF C-47s unloading at Tempelhof. (Albert Grandolini)

USAF Fairchild C-82 Packet arrives at Tempelhof in West Berlin. (Albert Grandolini)

departed from RAF Waterbeach, north-east of Cambridge for RAF Wunstorf, a few miles from Hannover in the British Zone, with three of them arriving in Berlin that night, making the first British deliveries in the relief effort.

By the following Monday, 28 June, the authorities made the decision to begin supplying the civilian population as well and the airlift, as history remembers it, began in earnest. On the first day, 87 C-47 flights of the US 60th Troop Carrier Group delivered 250 tons of supplies to the city. The RAF also made 21 flights, delivering 59 tons.

General LeMay announced that Allied aircraft would fly around the clock, seven days a week 'on a wartime basis', with the objective of delivering 30,000 tons of food and fuel to the city during the month of July. Two thirds would be flown by the USAF, the rest by the RAF.

On the 29 June, LeMay appointed Brigadier General Joseph Smith as commander of a special airlift task force. The first order he received from his boss, General LeMay was 'Insure [sic] that the maximum number of missions are flown and that optimum over-all efficiency of operation is maintained…' It was Smith who christened the American effort Operation Vittles, 'vittles' being an old-fashioned word for food. Now the operation had grown in scope beyond resupplying the British garrison, the RAF realised that Knicker (as in female underwear) was not really appropriate for a very public military operation.[9] Some bright spark suggested the less risqué Carter Paterson, the name of a popular British furniture removals firm, until Soviet propaganda pointed out that the British must be abandoning the city as they had hired such a firm. On 19 July, the British relief effort became Operation Plainfare, a much safer bet. The German's called it *Die Luftbrüke* (the Air Bridge) while the Soviets called it 'Die Bluff-Brücke'! They only expected the resupply effort to be needed for a few weeks.

The Aircraft

They may have had a massive support network behind them, but it was the aircraft and the brave and skilful air crew who were the heroes of the Berlin Airlift. The post-war draw-down had diminished the military fleet based in Germany so the planners had their work cut out to get sufficient aircraft as the tonnage requirement grew. The USAF immediately mobilised its relatively small C-47 fleet and concentrated them at the US bases close to the southern corridor, Rhein-Main and Wiesbaden. The RAF also quickly deployed all the available aircraft to airfields in their sector. This small fleet of transports began the deliveries into the city and the Berlin Airlift began.

From the moment the decision was made to begin the airlift, a global search began to acquire suitable transport aircraft, with favours being called in and heavyweight lobbying in the corridors of power in London and Washington. General Tunner , who would take over at the end of July, summed up the situation very succinctly: 'the key to the whole problem is big airplanes and lots of them!' His Military Air Transport Service (MATS) operation pulled aircraft from air bases in mainland USA and overseas, from as far as Alaska, Hawaii, Newfoundland and the Caribbean. Many senior USAF officers suddenly found themselves without their personal transports as a result of the trawl and aircraft were suddenly diverted from other deployments, much to the annoyance of their intended commanders.

France played a very small part in the operation, apart from managing the handling at Tegel, as most of their air transport fleet were tied up with their operations in Indochina. The only French aircraft recorded was an ex-Luftwaffe Ju 52/3m, which served in a communication role.

Thankfully there was very little attrition through accidents, but there were many problems of serviceability as a result of the hours flown and the unfavourable conditions, but the airlift planners needed more and more aircraft to satisfy the needs of the people of Berlin.

In the end, 689 different aircraft flew in the airlift; 441 US, 147 British and 101 British civilian contractors.

THE BASES

The airlift operation was going to be a major logistical challenge and therefore needed a network of bases and airfields that could service the anticipated volume of flights. It made sense to utilise the European rail network to transport supplies from the North Sea ports and from other friendly countries to staging bases across West Germany. From these bases, which for the most part were former Luftwaffe airfields, the daily shuttle along the air corridors could begin.[10]

Bases in the American Zone

Rhein-Main

Located near Frankfurt in the American Zone, the airfield started out as a launch pad for German airship operations in the 1930s,

including the *Graf Zeppelin* and the ill-fated *Hindenburg*. It was then used by the Luftwaffe during the Second World War (although it was badly bombed). Immediately after the war, it was operated as a US fighter base, before becoming the European terminal for the USAF Military Air Transport Service (MATS) in 1945 and thus the 'Gateway to Europe' for thousands of US troops. It had a single 6,000ft x 150ft (1,829m x 46m) concrete runway, with dispersed fighter-style hardstands on either side. Facilities clearly needed to be quickly upgraded so a major expansion programme was promptly initiated, creating 850,000 sq. ft. (78,968m²) of PSP hardstanding, 330,980 sq. ft. (30,749m²) of PSP parking apron, a network of PSP taxiways and gravelled roads, and the renovation/construction of accommodation. A second 7,000ft x 200ft runway was started and was 20 percent complete when the airlift came to an end. The improvements were geared around the needs of the C-54s, but C-47s also operated out of the base for a while. The airfield was upgraded with D2 high-intensity approach lighting in January 1949 and Krypton runway flash beacons in April 1949, making landing safer.

Table 3: Civilian and military aircraft used in the Berlin Airlift

Manufacturer	Aircraft	Notes
RAF		
Douglas	Dakota	British version of C-47
Avro	York	
Handley Page	Hastings	Entered service 1948
Short	Sunderland	Flying boat
USAF/USN		
Douglas	C-47 Skytrain	
Douglas	C-54 Skymaster	
Douglas	C-74 Globemaster	
Fairchild	C-82 Packet	
Boeing	C-97 Stratofreighter	Heavy lift duty
Douglas	R5D	USN version of C-54
France		
Junkers	Ju 52/3m	Armée de l'Air
Civilian		
Douglas	Dakota	British version of C-47 (19 used)
Avro	Lancastrian	Former Lancaster (17 used)
Handley Page	Halton	Former Halifax (41 used)
Avro	Tudor	Used as tanker (9 used)
Short	Hythe	Civilian version of Sunderland (3 used)
Consolidated	Liberator	(3 used)
Bristol	Freighter	All-passenger version known as Wayfarer. Otherwise heavy lift (6 used)
Vickers	Viking	(2 used)
Avro	York	(3 used)
Avro	Lincoln	(1 used)

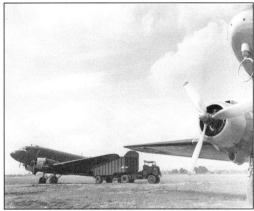

C-47 aircraft used in the Berlin Airlift task force at the Wiesbaden air base being loaded with food and supplies for the people of the Soviet-blockaded city of Berlin, 18 August 1948. (Byers via Truman Library)

C-47 aircraft loaded with food and supplies for the people of the Soviet-blockaded city of Berlin lined up and waiting to take off at Wiesbaden, 18 August 1948. (Byers via Truman Library)

Wiesbaden

Wiesbaden became a Luftwaffe fighter base in 1938 and was used throughout the Second World War for both fighters and bombers. It was occupied by American troops in 1945 and became a USAF base and the home of Headquarters US Air Force in Europe (USAFE). It had a 5,500ft x 120ft (1,676m x 37m) concrete runway with similar hardstands and taxiways. As with Rhein-Main, an immediate upgrade programme was initiated, extending the runway by 1,500ft (457m), creating 593,300 sq. ft. (55,119m²) of PSP apron and an additional 620,220 sq. ft. (57,620m²) of hardstanding, an extensive network of PSP or concrete taxiways and access roads. The base also got a new 166 x 88ft hanger and a host of other buildings and facilities. The airfield was upgraded with D2 high-intensity approach lighting in April 1949 and Krypton flashing runway beacons in May 1949. During the airlift, it was used initially by USAF C-47s and then by C-54s and C-82s. Interestingly, it was to be home to U-2 aircraft in 1950s, operating top secret reconnaissance flights over Eastern Europe.

BASES IN THE BRITISH ZONE[11]

Bückeburg

The air base was built in 1946 as RAF Bückeburg, serving the headquarters of the Royal Air Force Germany in Bad Eilsen. It complemented the nearby headquarters of the British Army of the Rhine in Bad Oeynhausen. Early on in the airlift it was used for fuel tanker operations by civilian Lancastrians run by Flight Refuelling Ltd.

Celle

Built in 1935 near Hannover as a Luftwaffe training base and taken over by the RAF after the war. Following the success of operating C-54s out of Faßberg, on 24 September 1948, the British agreed for the Americans to operate out of Celle too. The British installed new landing lights, improved accommodation and laid a new 5,400ft x 150ft (1,646m x 46m) tarmac runway and 1,980,999 sq. ft. (184,000m²) of PSP loading and maintenance apron. The airfield became operational 16 December, incorporating lessons learnt from the other airlift airfields, but unlike the US airfields, it used the new Calvert Bar System approach lights to guide the aircraft down. Unlike Faßberg, the British remained in charge of the base and operations. C-54s from Celle flew into Gatow up until 1 September 1949. Celle was viewed as the best of the supply airfields from an operational point of view.

Faßberg

An ex-Luftwaffe technical training base built in 1936, 50 miles south of Hamburg. Became an RAF fighter station after the war. By mid-July 1948, Wunstorf was getting dangerously crowded with airlift traffic, so all British Dakota operations moved to Faßberg, and operated out of there until 29 August. Some civilian operator twin-engined aircraft used the base between 4 and 28 August. In August, the decision was made to move some American C-54s to Faßberg in order to use this bigger aircraft on the shorter route to Berlin, saving an hour's flying time on each trip. The base already had a relatively new post-war 6,000ft x 150ft (1,829m x 46m) concrete runway but needed a major upgrade to accommodate C-54s. In just four weeks British Army engineers and local German labour built:

- A new 1,500,000 sq. ft. (140,000m²) of PSP loading area
- 0.9 mile (1.4km) of roads
- A 33ft (10m) wide, 1,894,448 sq. ft. (176,000m²) tarmac apron in front of the hangers
- Laid 5 miles (8km) of new rail track for sidings
- Installed airfield lighting
- Built accommodation for 3,000 extra personnel

The Americans remained unhappy, however, and the personnel stationed there complained bitterly about the standards of British food, accommodation, and recreation facilities.

The base continued to work within the BAFO organisation, although an American was in overall command. The C-54s operated there from 21 August 1948 to 1 September 1949. Faßberg was to specialise in delivering coal. In December, Faßberg started flying to Tegel, freeing up capacity for Gatow, which began taking volume traffic from Celle. The airfield was upgraded with D2 high-intensity approach lighting in March 1949.

Finkenwerder/Havel Lake

A specific feature of Berlin's landscape proved very useful for the airlift – the River Havel in the British sector opened up into a wide lake that was perfect for flying boat operations. From 5 July, RAF Coastal Command Short Sunderlands began operating from the old Blohm and Voss seaplane base at Finkenwerder on the River Elbe by Hamburg. The River Elbe was dangerous to operate on, still being strewn with half-submerged wartime wreckage and ground facilities were very basic indeed – a series of muddy tents by the water's edge and a hastily built hut on the back of a barge. The majestic flying boats would land on the Havel to be unloaded on to barges, DUKW amphibious vehicles and small boats.[12]

RAF Short S.25 Sunderland unloads food on the River Havel, Berlin 1948. (Sunderland Trust)

They became very proficient at unloading, and a whole Sunderland could be unloaded in 12 minutes. The pilots had been chasing submarines in the Irish Sea only days before and had to quickly adapt to a very different type of flying. The Sunderlands were joined by two civilian Short Hythe flying boats (the civilian version of the Sunderland), owned by Aquila Airways, in early August. This unusual delivery method lasted until 16 December 1948, when the river iced up, stopping the flying boats from landing.

Fuhlsbüttel

Hamburg's pre-war municipal airport, then operated by the RAF post-war as a transport hub. From 5 October 1948, Fuhlsbüttel became a major base for the civilian contractors, having relocated from Lübeck. Their freight included bulk liquid fuel in specially converted tankers using existing bulk storage tanks at the airfield. An additional runway was built at Fuhlsbüttel opening in December 1948 that was fully equipped for night landings. Operations continued there until 15 August 1949.

Lübeck

Built in 1935 as a Luftwaffe bomber base for He 111s. It later became a training station and then home to Ju 88 night-fighters, and Fw 190 and Me 262 fighters, before being taken over by the RAF. RAF Dakotas were moved there from 20 August until 23 September 1949 along with civilian contractor twin-engined aircraft from 28 August to 5 October 1948. It also became a major passenger terminal, rotating the Berlin Garrison and bringing people out of the city. The facilities at Lübeck were extensively improved during the operation: extending the concrete runway; laying around 880,000 sq. ft. (81,755m²) of PSP for unloading and aircraft parking; expanding the access road

network; installing a Calvert Approach Lighting system; and upgrading the area lighting for loading/unloading.

Schleswigland

Built as a glider club in 1936 and taken over by the Luftwaffe in 1938. During the war, He 111, Me 110, Ju 88 and Fw 190 aircraft operated there, mostly in the night-fighter role. Towards the end of the war the Me 262 jet fighter was also based there. The RAF then took over Schleswigland, running it as a fighter station and airborne forces training camp. A concrete runway was laid early in 1948, so it was the ideal location for an airlift base. With the arrival of the RAF Hastings in November/December and the extra capacity they brought, the British reserve airfield at Schleswigland was brought out of mothballs and extensively upgraded, becoming operational on 11 November 1948 and running through to 5 October 1949. Four civilian charter companies also worked out of there from 25 November 1948 through to 16 August 1949, being one of the three departure points for bulk liquid fuels distribution on Haltons and Liberators. Thankfully, Schleswigland already had bulk fuel tanks built by the Luftwaffe that could be adapted for use by the four-engined tankers.

Wunstorf

Built in 1934, Wunstorf was originally a Luftwaffe bomber base but became a fighter (single and twin-engined) base in 1940, then becoming an RAF fighter base. The base comprised two concrete runways, with taxiways and some concrete aprons in front of hangers, although the aircraft had to park on the grass. July 1948 experienced some awful weather and the grass quickly turned to mud, so that engineers had to be brought in to lay 5,100ft (1,554m) of PSP hardstands, which they completed in just four weeks. In addition, personnel accommodation was added, and rail sidings improved. Dakotas were stationed there between 25 June and 29 July 1948, and Yorks from 3 July to 29 August. From 4 August through to 15 August 1949, Wunstorf became one of three main bases for the onward distribution of bulk liquid fuels by the four-engined tankers of the British civilian contractors.

Initially, the fuel handling was very makeshift, which took time, was wasteful and very dangerous. By April 1949, bulk underground tanks had been installed so fuel could be pumped straight from the incoming trains into the tanks and then pumped straight to the aircraft at 100 gallons (455 litres) per minute. An average of 70,000 gallons (318,226 litres) a day passed through this set-up. In September 1948, a Calvert Approach Lighting system was installed, making low-visibility landing much safer.

Avro Yorks and Tudor at RAF Wunstorf. (Avro Museum)

Queue of Avro Yorks awaiting departure at RAF Wunstorf. (Albert Grandolini)

AIRFIELDS IN BERLIN

Gatow

Pre-war, Gatow was the main Luftwaffe training base, the equivalent of Cranwell in the UK, and served as a fighter base during the war. Located in the British sector, it had a 4,500ft (1,372m) PSP runway, and a 6,000ft x 150ft (1,829m x 46m) concrete runway was under construction, although incomplete when the airlift began. It finally opened on 17 July, much improving Gatow's capacity. The original PSP runway was re-laid in concrete after the metal planking was ripped up by a USAF Boeing C-97 Stratofreighter. Gatow became an

important destination for bulk fuels, flown by British civilian contractors. A special receiving system was installed with five large underground tanks and 18 aircraft bays set in a circular island in the middle of the airfield, plus floodlights allowing unloading to operate 24 hours per day. It began operating in March 1949 and could unload 14 tanker aircraft simultaneously. Unlike the US airfields, Gatow was installed with the new Calvert Bar Approach Lighting System to guide the pilots onto the runway.

Tegel

Tegel was built from scratch on a patch of waste ground earmarked for allotment gardens in the French sector of Berlin.[13] Work began on 8 August 1948 and around 17,000 Berliners worked on the project under the supervision of US engineers. It took them 93 days to build a 5,500ft x 150ft (1,676m x 46m) runway, using crushed rubble taken from bombed out buildings mixed with asphalt and ballast taken from disused railway lines. In addition to the runway, 120,000 sq. ft. (11,148m^2) of apron was built, 6,020ft (1,835m) of taxiways, between 50ft and 120ft in width, all from a similar construction. A network of access roads and rail sidings was also completed, along with administration and operations buildings, a control tower, a fire station and a hospital. A

BABS (Blind Approach Beacon System) was installed by the British. It cost 17,879,218 D-Marks at 1948 prices.

Learning from the deficiencies of the other Berlin airfields, the designers were able to 'design-out' most of the problems thus ensuring a smooth operation from day one. General Tunner insisted that the new runway be laid in the same direction as the other Berlin airfields to minimise risk of collision. The first aircraft to land was a C-54 on 5 November, and the airfield became fully operational on 16 December, being used by USAF, RAF and civilian contractors. Pilots complained that a 200ft (61m) tall radio mast used by the Soviets to broadcast their propaganda station, Berlin Rundfunk, was a hazard for approaching aircraft. The French commander made an official request to the Soviets for the tower to be taken down, which was duly refused so he took matters into his own hands, sent a team of engineers over the sector border and promptly blew the tower up, a fact that is mysteriously omitted from the USAFE official report![14] The French supervised the unloading using local labour and handled all the other activities on the base, although a team of American and British Air Traffic Controllers ran the tower. Tegel was served by the northern corridor, so it was sensible that it became a destination for bulk liquid fuels flown in by British civilian contractors. Being able to start with a clean sheet, the engineers built huge underground storage tanks that connected directly to the aircraft. The fuel was then pumped to a distribution point at Plötzensee. The airfield was upgraded with D2 high-intensity approach lighting in March 1949 and Krypton flashing runway beacons in April 1949 and a second runway was opened just as the airlift came to an end.

Tempelhof

Tempelhof in the American sector was Berlin's pre-war civilian airport but not for the faint-hearted, with the final approach skimming the rooftops of nearby apartment buildings and dodging a tall chimney. Tempelhof embodied elegant 1930s air travel but was hardly suitable for large scale logistics operations. It had impressive crescent shaped terminal buildings (with seven stories underground) and a wide curved apron made from blocks of marble for unloading aircraft but lacked any concrete runways, the Americans having laid a 4,987ft x 120ft (1,520m x 37m) PSP on rubber matting runway in 1945, with some dispersed fighter-style hardstands.[15]

Aircraft landed on the PSP, but still took off from grass, which became a field of mud in bad weather. The runway also began to break up under the volume of traffic, so was reinforced with a mixture of coarse sand and grit, hot tar and asphalt. On 8 July, the Americans began building a second runway at Tempelhof. It was to be 5,750ft x 140ft (1,753m x 43m) and made from PSP and PAP over asphalt over crushed rubble – the planking was shipped over from the US and the asphalt over from the British or American Zones, but Berlin had plenty of brick rubble available!

These construction requirements took up 75 to 80 tons of the daily airlift capacity, but it was a necessary additional burden. The runway was ready to use on 12 September, greatly adding to Tempelhof's capacity. They then began a third 6,150ft x 140ft (1,875m x 43m) runway, made from heavier asphalt with no PSP and this was completed in late November, just as Germany's bitter winter was closing in. The installation of D2 high-intensity approach lighting completed in April 1949 (albeit right through a cemetery) and

C-54 lands at Tempelhof. (Albert Grandolini)

A bulldozer building new runway at Tempelhof. (US Army Military History Institute)

Bristol Freighter from Silver City Airways with RAF Avro Yorks in the background, at RAF Wunstorf. (Avro Museum)

C-47 aircraft used in the Berlin Airlift task force at the Wiesbaden air base being loaded with food and supplies for the people of the Soviet-blockaded city of Berlin. Trucks containing supplies are driven out to load the aircraft, 18 August 1948. (Byers via Truman Library)

as wheel chocks, starter trollies and petrol bowsers.[16] Large and heavy equipment was flown-in in special heavy-lift aircraft such as the Bristol Freighter, including bulldozers and fire engines.

The British Army set up an Army Air Transport Organisation at Wunstorf on 28 June 1948, comprising a Royal Army Service Corps (RASC) Rear Airfield Supply organisation at Wunstorf and a Forward Airfield Supply organisation at Gatow.[17] These were responsible for collecting the supplies, storing them, preparing them for shipment and loading them on the aircraft, and at the other end, unloading them into the hands of the West Berlin Magistrat/Senat (City Authorities).[18]

To start with, there was limited handling equipment available, so virtually every item shipped had to be manhandled on and off trains, aircraft and vehicles as it passed through the supply chain. As the operation developed, it was discovered that men could actually load and unload quicker than by using forklifts and cranes, so the airlift remained a predominantly manual handling exercise. Over time, it was determined that six-man teams should unload the rail freight on to trucks. The trucks would then drive (ideally a short distance) right up to the aircraft, where ten-man teams transferred the supplies onto the aircraft.

After flying along the corridors and landing at one of the two (and later three) airfields in West Berlin, 12-man crews would unload the supplies from the aircraft onto trucks for onward distribution across the city.

With military personnel supervising, most of the labour was provided by the West German Länder (States) and the West Berlin Magistrat/Senat and comprised mostly Eastern European refugees and some Berliners. Their hard work was rewarded by improved rations and steady pay. Over time, the loading and unloading got faster and faster as the teams settled into the task. In the first few chaotic weeks it took around five hours to load a C-47 but with practice, they were able to average an amazing ten minutes per aircraft. Unloading could take from 8 to 45 minutes but averaged around 30 minutes.

Some of the supplies had difficult handling requirements. Coal was a particular problem, being heavy and very messy, but needed in large quantities to generate electricity, to power the city's water and

Krypton runway flash beacons in June 1949, made landing at night and in poor weather much safer.

Many of the bases that served the airlift went on to become Cold War military bases or major civilian airports.

Airlift Operations

The logistical organisation and infrastructure had to play catchup with the chaotic early days of the airlift. Engineers had to rapidly construct roads, taxiways, fuel stores, pipelines, lighting, hard standings for loading, aircrew accommodation, unloading, handling and maintenance facilities, patch up and lengthen runways and connect the airfields to the railway network – all against the elements and in an island city that was still picking itself up after the war. The early operations also suffered shortages of basic ground equipment, such

C-54 Aircraft being unloaded at Tempelhof. (Albert Grandolini)

sewage system, as well as heat public buildings and homes. Before coming up with an ideal solution, they experimented with various ways of transporting it, including loading up the bomb bays of huge RAF Lincoln and USAF B-29 Superfortress bombers, flying over an empty part of the city and dumping the coal from the air in one black deluge.[19] This was tried over what would become Tegel Airfield in the French Sector, with the coal disintegrating on impact, covering the onlookers in coal dust. The solution turned out to be wonderfully low-tech. There were huge numbers of war surplus GI duffel bags in storage in Germany, and these were ideal to move the coal in manageable loads, while minimising dust.[20] The first load of 200 duffel bags full of coal was brought in by C-54 on 7 July, with the RAF's first trip being made on 19 July. The bags were re-used countless times, and every spilt piece of coal and speck of coal dust was carefully swept up by teams of German women. The ultimate solution for coal shipments was lightweight four-ply paper sacks, that could only be re-used a few times, but the weight saving easily paid for them.

Flour being unloaded at Tempelhof under the watchful eye of a Military Policeman. (US Army Military History Institute)

Unloading cargo from a US Navy R5D at Tempelhof. (US National Archives via US Navy)

A US Air Force C-74 Globemaster aircraft touched down at RAF Gatow with more than 20 tons of flour from the United States, 19 August 1948. (US National Archives)

Liquid fuels and lubricants were also very difficult to handle – jerrycans or large drums were extremely heavy and would wreak havoc if they shifted in transit. The arrival of the civilian tanker aircraft solved this problem. Certain bases specialised in fuel handling and after a while it became very efficient, with fuel pumped from the arriving trains into huge underground storage tanks. Pipeline systems were then installed to take the fuel directly to the aircraft. At the other end, similar infrastructure was eventually installed, with fuel piped to the waiting tankers for onward distribution around the city.

Avro Tudor tanker of Airflight Ltd at RAF Gatow, with runway repairs going on in the foreground. (Avro Museum)

At the other end of the spectrum, the fresh fruit and vegetables delivered by the French daily to Rhein-Main proved particularly difficult to secure in the back of the aircraft. A load master described it as trying to lash down 'jelly'. The RAF experimented dropping loaves of bread from the bomb bay of a bomber over Gatow but it failed.

From a standing start, the airspace around Berlin and the corridors had become the busiest in the world and so the airlift planners had to invent and introduce new air traffic control systems to cope with the unprecedented volume of air traffic in order to avoid accidents. With the concentration of so many aircraft in one place, the risk of collision was high, but once the border into the Soviet Zone had been crossed along the three air corridors, any accident or incident would mean landing in hostile territory, with the constant threat of an international incident. The western sectors of Berlin were also very congested and completely surrounded by the Soviets, so strict air traffic control was essential there too.

US Navy R5D crewmembers are briefed for the flight at Intelligence and Briefing by an Air Force captain. Here they receive information on Soviet activity in the corridor, the weather expected en route, and any special route instructions, 5 October 1949. (US National Archives via US Navy)

The early days of the airlift were chaotic, with a free-for-all up and down the corridors in answer to the 'do all you can' effort. At peak times, aircraft were arriving every few minutes and bad weather could quickly disrupt landings, creating a real danger of mid-air and ground collisions. It was not long, therefore, before cooler heads prevailed, and some degree of order was established, aided by the arrival of a number of professional US Civil Aeronautics Administration (CAA) air traffic controllers. Versions of the systems they developed to handle

USAF officers converse in front of a map showing the air corridors into West Berlin. (Albert Grandolini)

along the central corridor, dropping down back to base. At the same time, the British were using the short central corridor for both inbound and outbound traffic from their base at Wunstorf, near Hannover, so aircraft were approaching each other head on, never an ideal situation even if they may have been delineated by height with the British below 8,000ft (2,438m), the Americans above it. The Sunderlands were the first aircraft to use the northern corridor from their river base near Hamburg and when the British Dakota fleet moved to Faßberg at the end of July 1948, they also began to use the northern corridor, and the central corridor became only for eastbound (homebound) aircraft.

Peacetime regulations were quickly side-lined by a fairly robust intervention from General Smith, and he began a series of experiments to optimise the flow of aircraft. His successor, General Tunner, took these efficiencies to a whole new level. The most basic control was via height and time, where aircraft were despatched at fixed time intervals and at specific altitudes. Smith slashed the time separation allowing aircraft to land at four-minute intervals (ten minutes at night) and implemented a complex arrangement of five height specific flight paths: at 5,000; 6,000; 7,000; 8,000; 9,000; and 10,000 feet. After a while, the 1,000ft separation was reduced to 500ft.

When Tunner came on board, he immediately reduced the flight levels to three, and finally to two, thus considerably improving flight safety but also simplifying the approach to Berlin. The flight levels were as follows:

- From Rhein-Main and Wiesbaden: 5,000 and 6,000ft (1,524 and 1,829m)
- From Wunstorf and Lübeck: 3,500 and 5,500ft (1,067 and 1,676m)
- From Celle: 4,000 and 4,500ft (1,219 and 1,372m)
- From Faßberg: 2,000 and 2,500ft (610 and 762m)
- The central return corridor operated at 6,500 and 7,500ft (1,981 and 2,286m)

the huge volume of traffic, such as using slat boards to monitor aircraft and their stacking patterns are still used in air traffic control today.

The Americans established a pattern of flying to Berlin along the southern corridor from their bases around Frankfurt, and returned

From early July, both the British and the Americans began using a 'block' system, where they avoided delays caused by aircraft flying at different speeds by sending a single type of aircraft down the corridor from a particular base at a particular time and at a particular height. Each aircraft had to hit the radio navigation beacons within a 30 second window. Once the last of the 'block' of one particular type had taken off, then the first of the next 'block' was despatched, continuing in a cycle throughout the day. The parameters were tweaked over time to get the optimum mix. In order to achieve this level of precision, all aircraft flew under Instrument Flight Rules (IFR), regardless of the weather.[21]

One simple innovation was the adoption of a simple decodable call-sign system for US pilots to use over the airwaves

Lt. General William H. Tunner. (US Air Force)

Two USAF C-54s in flight. (Albert Grandolini)

Navigating the air corridors in a US Navy R5D. (US National Archives via US Navy)

Air Communications (AACS) Wing began upgrading the navigation and communication infrastructure for all of the airlift routes. Radio beacons were used as navigational waypoints and Radio Ranges were an excellent way of funnelling aircraft into the corridors and on runway approach. Ground Control Approach (GCA) radar sets would allow ground-based personnel to talk down aircraft over the radio. The AACS also improved voice radio communication, adding additional channels to avoid congestion and improving landlines. Pilots would take the routes as shown in Table 4.

Early in the airlift, the planners tried to make the corridors one-way, for obvious safety reasons. This was maintained for the busier Central and Southern corridors but as the demand for flights increased and new bases were opened, it made sense to allow two-way traffic along the northern corridor, with aircraft carefully delineated by height. The northern corridor therefore carried Berlin-bound traffic from Faßberg, Celle, Wunstorf, Fuhlsbüttel, Lübeck, Schleswigland and Finkenwerder, which would head for the RRS and beacons at Dannenberg and Restorf, before entering the corridor. It would also carry return traffic for Lübeck, Fuhlsbüttel, Schleswigland and Finkenwerder. Both flows had to watch out for the beautiful but lumbering Sunderland flying boats flying at 1,000ft, who cruised slightly faster than the venerable C-47, but considerably slower than the Hastings, Yorks, Tudors and Lancastrians. This problem was removed in December 1948 when the flying boat operation was cancelled because of ice. Flight level 3,000ft was reserved for aircraft in distress in either direction and all the runways in the network operated from east to west, thus reducing the danger of collision.

These routes worked successfully over more than 275,000 trips, running 24/7 in all weathers with very few mishaps – a master class in precision flying and disciplined air traffic control.

Before the blockade, approximately 12,000 tons of supplies were being shipped on a daily basis into the city by rail, barge and by road.

with the various control towers. C-54s became 'Big' while C-47s were 'Little'. Eastbound aircraft were 'Easy' and westbound aircraft became 'Willie'. Each aircraft also had a unique identifier. So, C-47 number 1234, flying eastwards along the corridor towards Tempelhof became 'Little Easy 1234' and anyone on that frequency knew exactly who they were and where they were going.[22]

Navigation aids were in their infancy, but those wartime innovations were severely tested by the scale of the airlift requirement. Initially, the technology was basic, with a limited number of installations available, but as the airlift got more organised, the US Airways and

Table 4: Route from Rhein-Main or Wiesbaden in the American Zone to Tempelhof in Berlin.

Outbound (to Berlin)
Taking off from Rhein-Main, turn left, climb to assigned altitude of 900ft and proceed to the first Radio Beacon Waypoint at Darmstadt.
Taking off from Wiesbaden, turn left and proceed to the first Radio Beacon Waypoint at Darmstadt but at 4,000ft.
Now part of the integrated traffic flow, proceed to the Radio Beacon Waypoint at Aschaffenberg, turning left towards the Radio Range Station (RRS) at Fulda, maintaining a constant gap between the aircraft and those ahead and behind.
Enter the Southern Corridor over the Soviet Zone at Fulda, steering by dead reckoning, before picking up the Tempelhof RRS for an accurate fix.
Approaching Tempelhof, now guided by the Air Traffic Controller's instructions, turning left at the Tempelhof Radio Beacon, descending in strict order to 2,000ft by the time of reaching the Wedding Radio Beacon.
Turning right at Wedding and dropping to 500ft, two more right-hand turns bring the aircraft right in line with the runway for a straight-in approach from six miles out.
Approaching the runway at 120 miles an hour and 400ft, if visibility was a mile or better and the cloud base over 400ft, land. If not, abort the landing, returning along the central corridor to base.
Return (to Wiesbaden or Rhein-Main)
From Tempelhof, the pilot would head west south-west towards the Radio Beacon at Wannsee, thus avoiding any traffic from Gatow, just to the north.
The aircraft would now join the central corridor and proceed by dead reckoning towards the Radio Range Station at Braunschweig.
It would then turn left towards the Fritzlar Radio Beacon.
To head to Wiesbaden, bear right following the Wiesbaden Radio Beacon and turn right on approach.
For Rhein-Main, bear left at Fritzlar and then head for the Radio Beacon at Staden. Then on to the Radio Beacon and RRS at Rhein-Main.

Table 5: Route from Faßberg in the British Zone to Gatow in Berlin.

Outbound (from Faßberg to Gatow or Tegel)
Taking off from Faßberg, the pilot would head for the Radio Range Station and Beacon at Dannenberg, which served the same role as the RRS at Fulda, as the entry point to the northern corridor across Soviet territory. RAF aircraft would also have the Eureka beacon at Restorf as a waypoint just before the border.
The pilot would then proceed down the northern corridor. RAF aircraft could also use Gee to confirm their position.
Having safely navigated through the corridor, the pilot would then lock onto the RRS and Radio Beacon at Lubars/Frohnau.
At Lubars/Fronhau, for Gatow, the pilot would turn right for Gatow's Radio Beacon before landing, as per the Tempelhof rules. For Tegel, he would bear left at Lubars/Fronhau, head to the Tegel beacon and make his approach.
Return (from Gatow/Tegel to Faßberg)
After leaving Gatow (or Tegel), the pilot would head westward along the central corridor heading for the extra Radio Beacon north of Braunschweig. This was an addition to the airlift operation, separating Faßberg traffic from Celle/Wunstorf traffic.
Then turn right towards the Dedelsdorf Radio Beacon.
The aircraft would then go on to land at Faßberg.

Table 6: Breakdown of tonnage delivered during the Airlift. (Tunner, Report on the Airlift Berlin Mission)

Item	Quantity (tons)	Source/Comment
Coal	3,084	West Germany
Food	1,435	West Germany and other European countries
Including:		
Flour	646	USA, Hungary and Denmark
Potatoes*	180	West Germany, US, UK and Holland
Fruit and vegetables	144	
Cereals	125	
Meat and fish**	109	Norway (fish)
Sugar	85	
Fats	64	
Salt	19	
Coffee***	11	
Milk*	5	Holland, Belgium, Denmark, Switzerland
Yeast	3	
Commerce and Industrial supplies	255	
Newsprint	35	For newspaper printing
Liquid fuel	16	
Medical supplies	2	
Military supplies	763	
Passenger flights	30	
Total	5,620	

* Potatoes and milk were dehydrated to save weight.
** To save weight, meat was de-boned. Meat and fish were brought in fresh and frozen, and the transit was so quick that frozen items did not have time to defrost.
*** It was more efficient to bring in real coffee than use fuel to make the ersatz coffee that Berliners were used to.

Navigation

Accurate navigation was essential for airlift operations – the skies were full of aircraft to avoid and straying into Soviet controlled airspace risked being shot down or causing an international incident. Technology had come on leaps and bounds during the Second World War but the systems available were unsophisticated compared to modern avionics. However, they were key to the success of the airlift.

The aids can be broken down into three areas: for navigation; for approach and landing and for airspace management.

Aids for navigation

Rather than just rely on traditional navigation techniques of a map, compass and stopwatch, in the crowded contentious airspace of the airlift, modern (for the time) navigation aids were employed – some fixed and some mobile.

The low frequency Non-Directional radio Beacon (NDB) was the most common system used during the airlift. Base stations dotted around West Germany and West Berlin broadcast a low frequency signal on a set wavelength. Initially the ground component was mounted on the back of a truck, but later the equipment was mounted on 5ft (1.5m) high platforms, creating a more permanent set-up. It was rigged up to a substantial antenna set-up, comprising masts and long trailing wires which would be staked to the ground in a particular pattern.

It was easy to use and was normally reliable, although it was not robust enough for the volume of traffic experienced with the airlift. The broadcasts were omni-directional, that is, broadcast in a 360-degree arc and operated 24/7 as a homing beacon for transiting aircraft.

Navigation around the end of the central corridor was much improved by the installation of a Radio Beacon at Braunschweig in the British Zone, while the route to Gatow was helped by the installation of a beacon at Frohnau in the French Sector, just north of what would become Tegel Airfield. The southern corridor also benefited from the installation of a Beacon at Darmstadt, acting as a rallying point for aircraft departing Wiesbaden and Rhein-Main.

In September 1948, arrangements were made to replace the mobile units with T-5 beacons from the US and these became operational in February 1949, improving the reliability of these key navigation aids.

The ground-based NDB was used in conjunction with an Automatic Direction Finder (ADF) in the aircraft. The kit comprised a Radio Compass Unit, the direction indicator on the instrument panel and the distinctive loop antenna contained in an aerodynamic teardrop fairing fitted to the outside of the aircraft. On pre-Second World War aircraft, there was a loop aerial on the top of the fuselage that the operator could rotate to fine-tune the signal. The operator tuned the Radio Compass Unit to the correct frequency for the beacon they were looking for, and the Radio Magnetic Indicator (RMI) on the instrument panel automatically moved a compass-like pointer to show the direction of the beacon, allowing the pilot to adjust his heading accordingly. The beacon could also be used for an instrument approach to a runway.

The British used a couple of systems that had proved invaluable during the Second World War. Eureka/Rebecca was designed to allow pathfinder paratroopers and special operations to direct further air drops to their precise location. Eureka was the ground part of the system and Rebecca was fitted in the aircraft. Eureka sent out a series of radio pulses which were picked up by the aircraft's antennas. The Rebecca unit calculated the range to the Eureka based on the timing of the return signals, and its relative position using a highly directional antenna. The signal was sent to a scope in the aircraft, which the navigator 'interpreted' giving heading corrections to the pilot. The system provided continuous coverage up to 20 miles at 1,500ft (32km at 457m) and up to 60 miles at 5,000ft (97km at 1,524m) and gave excellent results, with accurate position fixes being possible even under IFR conditions. Eureka beacons were located as navigational aids at key waypoints and also as a final turn indicator on the approach to Gatow.

The RAF aircraft also made use of the 'Central German Gee Chain', which was set up during the war to provide navigational guidance for bombers. A chain of Gee transmitters located in friendly territory sent out precisely timed pulses forming a series of invisible lines over Europe. Antennas on the aircraft picked up these signals, sending them to a black box on the navigator's table. The navigator looked at a series of blips on the box's oscilloscope display, twiddled various knobs to fine-tune the signals and took a series of readings, which when plotted on a chart, could provide a location fix. With a skilled operator and in favourable conditions, the 'fix' could be accurate to as little as 100 yards (91m), but in practice accuracy was ± 1 mile or more, decreasing the further away from the signal source, so other methods would be used to verify the location.

Much of this equipment was still on the secret list so was only available on military aircraft, with the civilian contractors relying on traditional navigational techniques, adding to the makeshift appearance of their operation.

That all stopped on 24 June 1948. It was an immense task to try to determine a 'shopping list' that accurately represents the daily needs of a city of 2.2 million people, and this was reflected in the early estimates of tonnage the airlift was expected to deliver. To start with, the airlift was given the vague brief of bringing in 'as much as possible' but soon the initial 'guesstimates' put the requirement at around 2,000 tons/day. As soon as coal was added to the mix, the expected tonnage rose rapidly, reaching 4,500 tons/day by the early August. This delivered a meagre 1,600 calories per person (increased to 1,880 in January 1949). The daily tonnage requirement increased to 5,000 tons/day in mid-September and by mid-October increased to 5,620 tons/day, reflecting the need for more coal as the winter closed in. This 5,620 tons included a dizzying array of goods, as may be expected for a large city. A typical day's shipment is shown in Table 6.

The daily manifests included every possible household and industrial item that could be imagined. Around 35 tons of newsprint, the huge rolls of paper used to print newspapers, was brought in every day, so the 'free' press in West Berlin could counter the aggressive propaganda spewing from the SMA. The shipments included mail, medical supplies, raw materials, construction materials, military equipment and liquid fuels and lubricants to keep the machines and vehicles going and vehicles themselves. Certain luxuries, such as tobacco, were included to maintain morale. Asphalt for runway construction was shipped over in smelly 400lb (181kg) drums. In all cases, the use of packaging material was minimised, which did result

Aids for approach and landing

Approach systems were used in two important roles during the airlift: funnelling the aircraft safely into the air corridors; and the more normal conventional role of directing aircraft onto the correct approach for landing.

Three Radio Range Stations (RRS) broadcast low frequency Radio Range signals to approaching aircraft; one on the approach to the US Rhein-Main airbase, one on the approach to the entrance of the southern air corridor at Fulda (by far the busiest corridor), and one on the approach to Tempelhof in West Berlin. A series of radio towers broadcast low frequency Morse signals for the letter 'A' and the letter 'N' on specific bearings, which were picked up by a receiver in the aircraft. The receiver played a tone through the pilot's headset or through a speaker in the cockpit. If the aircraft veered to the left of the required heading, they would hear the 'N' tone (dah-dit, dah-dit, ...) in their ear and would correct to the right. If they veered to the right of the heading, they had conversely hear the 'A' tone (dit-dah, dit-dah …) and would bear left. If they were on track, they would hear a steady tone, safe in the knowledge they were on the right heading.

There were several downsides to the low frequency systems being used, which became more apparent as the operation intensified. There was limited frequency spectrum available, which inevitably meant that ordinary radio broadcasts were disrupted. They were also very susceptible to interference from weather and jamming by the Soviets.

The solution was to move to very high frequency (VHF) based systems and in October 1948, a request was made to obtain six very high frequency VAR (Visual Aural Radio) Ranges from the US CAA (Civil Aeronautics Administration). CAA staff were flown in to install the systems and they were all up and running by the end of January 1949, located at:

> Fulda – zone side of the southern corridor
> Braunschweig – zone side of centre corridor
> Dannenberg – zone side of the northern corridor
> Tempelhof – Berlin side of southern corridor
> Lubars – Berlin side of northern corridor
> Wolfenbüttel – to project a beam perpendicular to the southern corridor as a check point

The VAR Range station sent out two different signals interpreted by the VHF receiver as a visual image on a dial located on the instrument panel, combining the A and N ranges as above, plus a yellow and blue quadrant. If on course, the pilot would hear a constant tone as above and the needle on the dial will be pointing between the colour quadrants. If the pilot deviated from the set course, he would hear either the A or N tone in his headset and the needle would point into one of the colour quadrants until corrected accordingly.[23]

Ground Controlled Approach (GCA) would then handle the final approach.[24] The main ground unit was housed in a shipping container-size box on the back of a trailer, with various protrusions acting as antenna. The trailers were painted in a red and white chequer board pattern for high visibility. Operators in headsets would stare into scopes, giving course corrections and 'talking down' the approaching aircraft to a safe landing.

The RAF used 'Blind Approach Beacon Systems' (BABS) at their airfields and at Tegel. Using similar principles to Eureka/Rebecca, they transmitted a series of dots on one side of the runway and a series of dashes on the other. The relative strength of these signals gave the aircraft's relative position to the centre line of the runway.

The final approach to the airfield was assisted by several visual systems. All of the runways used by the airlift were equipped with D-1 lighting, which worked well, although certain bases were upgraded to brighter Krypton condenser discharge runway lights in early 1949. At the same time, the US airfields were upgraded to high-intensity red and amber D-2 Gas Accumulator approach lighting, mounted on towers made from sections of PSP welded together. The British airfields at Celle and Gatow used a different system for approach lighting, the Calvert Bar System, which is still used at airports today. The Calvert system, named after Mr E.S. Calvert of the Royal Aircraft Establishment was developed in 1946 and featured a centre line of sodium lights leading up to the runway's threshold and a series of horizontal bars of lights, decreasing in width towards the threshold (a Christmas tree shape, with the pointed top being the threshold).

Aids for airspace management

Navigation into West Berlin got much easier with the installation of a CPS-5 search radar on top of the eight storey Airdrome building, completed on 27 December 1948. The CPS-5 was a medium weight transportable search radar developed by Bell Telephone Laboratories and General Electric designed for early warning and came into service in January 1945. It was operated by a crew of ten and could provide a solid search of up to 60 miles away and up to 40,000 feet (97km and 12,192m), more in ideal conditions and with a skilled operator. It featured an MTI (Moving Target Indicator), a video mapping unit (which super-imposed a map over the radar display), a large Skiatron display so the chief controller could monitor all traffic, several PPI (Planned Position Indicator) scopes and data boards made from edge lit Plexiglas – all cutting-edge technology at the time. This key addition gave controllers a good overview of the whole of Berlin's airspace, allowing them to smooth out the traffic flow into all three airfields in West Berlin in all weathers, and allowing the GCA operators to concentrate on talking down approaching aircraft. The system did not have any 'Identification Friend or Foe' (IFF) capability so controllers could check the nationality of the aircraft by ordering 45 degree turns to the left or right for 45 seconds and tracking them on the radar.

It is a testament to the navigation and safety systems put in place that in all the hundreds of thousands of take offs, climbs, cruises, manoeuvres, descents, approaches and landings, there were remarkably few accidents.

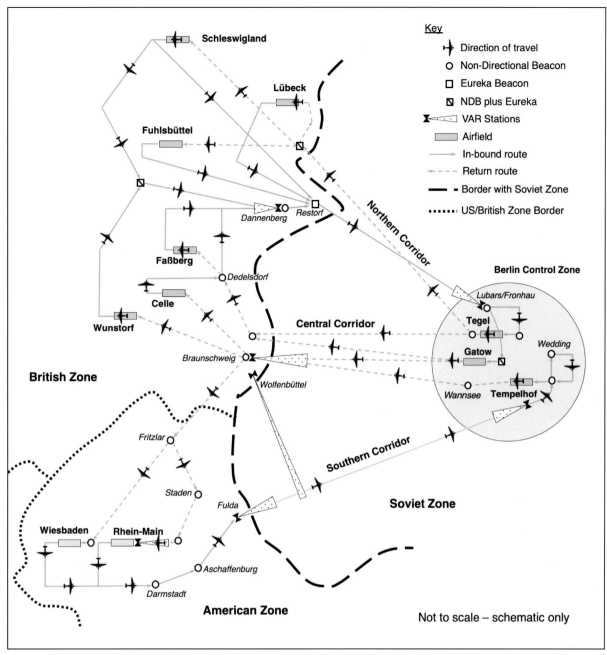

Schematic showing Airlift routes and navigation points. (Author)

Loading milk onto a C-47 at Wiesbaden destined for the people of West Berlin, 18 August 1948. (Byers via Truman Library)

Lashing down sacks of flour on a US Navy R5D. (US National Archives via US Navy)

USN R5D Skymasters, flown by navy fliers participating in the Berlin Airlift, are unloaded at Templehof, 5 October 1949. (US National Archives via US Navy)

Avro 691 Lancastrian C.Mk.II tanker 'Sky Empire' G-AKMW of Skyways Ltd. (Avro Museum)

in some damage of the goods, but this was more than offset by the weight saved. Pilferage was a constant problem, especially in Berlin, where goods had huge value on the black market.

In honour of the USAF's 1st birthday as a service independent of the US Army, on 18 September 1948, General Clay ordered a maximum effort focusing entirely on shipping coal. By the end of the day, aircraft from both forces had flown 897 missions (653 American, 244 British) and delivered 6,988 tons (5,583 American, 1,405 British), with aircraft landing on average every 96 seconds. The ground crew also set new records for loading and unloading. Whilst this level of activity was not sustainable for long, it demonstrated to the Soviets (and the world) that the Allies could supply the population of West Berlin indefinitely. For Stalin, it was perhaps the beginning of the end for his blockade.

Another high for the airlift was the famous 'Easter Parade' that took place between noon on Saturday 15 April and noon on Sunday 16 April 1949. Worried that the personnel involved in the operation were getting complacent, Clay ordered a maximum effort again focussed on a single cargo, coal, and set an optimistic target of 10,000 tons for that 24-hour period.[25] Harnessing the competitive nature of the various base commanders, the event energised the whole operation, from end to end. By lunchtime on Sunday, the Easter Parade had delivered 12,941 tons over 1,398 flights. On average, an aircraft was landing at one of Berlin's three airfields every 62 seconds. Not only was this event a huge publicity coup, but it also boosted the ongoing daily average from 6,300 tons in March to 7,850 tons in April and 8,000 tons in May and June. These figures were sending another devastating

message to Stalin that the Allies were keeping West Berlin open for business.

As well as developing the infrastructure within the city, a major planning and supply chain had to be established to get the supplies to the airfields. Most shipments from the US came via the Marinex express ocean service from ports in the New York area across to the port of Bremerhaven, in the northwest corner of Germany, while fuel tankers were diverted from plying their trade around the world to deliver to the airlift effort. The shipments were then sent on by rail to railheads near the relevant airfield, while coal came direct from the Ruhr by train. At the railheads, trucks would take the loads straight to the aircraft. The air bases would become major distribution hubs, receiving hundreds of thousands of tons of supplies and cross-loading them to the awaiting transports, mostly using local labour, happy to work for extra rations.

All US-sourced eastbound air freight was marshalled at Middletown Air Materiel Area (MAAMA) at Olmsted AFB, Pa, before being flown to Rhein-Main or Wiesbaden. Special rail links were set up between the air and sea hubs carrying urgent spare parts to the aircraft servicing depots in Bavaria.

The airlift turned out to be a truly international effort, with air crew and aircraft coming from all corners of the world. US Airforce Europe (USAFE) and British Air Forces of Occupation (BAFO) formed the initial fleet, but this was soon supplemented by RAF Transport Command from Great Britain, USAF Military Air Transport Service (MATS) based in the US and the US Navy.[26]

In addition, aircrew from the British dominions; Royal New Zealand Air Force (RNZAF), Royal Australian Air Force (RAAF) and Royal South African Air Force (RSAAF) began arriving from September onwards on six-month rotations. Interestingly, the Netherlands offered aircraft and aircrews, but the British refused on the ground that the agreement to use the air corridors was *only* for the four occupying powers. The Dutch had benefited from Allied airlifts during the Second World War so were keen to repay the favour.

The planners soon realised that the fleet of military aircraft was insufficient to deliver the amount of food the city required, so in late July they got the Foreign Office to approach civilian operators, who would quickly become a key part of the airlift. These were British companies and were mostly crewed by ex-RAF aircrew, which helped interoperability with their military counterparts to a certain degree, but they were a ragtag bunch, all working to their own procedures and standards which made it complicated to integrate them into rigid military routines. In a combination of gold rush fever and Dunkirk spirit, they threw themselves into the operation, with some of the aircraft being barely airworthy. It was not until March 1949 that British European Airways Corporation, the nationalised British European carrier, officially took on a coordinating role for the contractors and the operation became more business-like. Civilian operators such as Flight Refuelling Ltd, Skyways, Lancashire Aircraft Corporation and Bond Air Services flew a variety of aircraft, many converted from wartime British bombers and transports. The Avro Lancastrian, both in tanker and transport version, was the civilian version of the famous Lancaster bomber, while the Handley Page Halton was an ex-Halifax.

The first contract flight took place on 27 July 1948 by a Flight Refuelling Ltd Avro Lancastrian and a total of 25 different civilian operators would continue right through to August 1949, completing almost 22,000 sorties with a fleet of over 100 aircraft, bringing in almost 150,000 tons of much needed supplies. The civilian operators were given a lot of the hard-to-handle freight, so it did not interrupt military efficiency. They also specialised in the delivery of bulk liquid fuel to the extent that by early 1949, every vehicle in West Berlin was being run on fuel delivered by British civilian operators.[27]

As is often the case, the pilots tend to get all the glory, while the ground crew get little credit. In the case of the Berlin Airlift, it was the massive support and maintenance operation who were the unsung heroes. All the aircraft involved in the operation were designed for long haul operations; a normal take off, a long steady climb and cruise and then a gentle landing. Airlift flying was totally different, with numerous short hops each day at maximum – or often more than maximum – gross weights and with heavy landings on poor surfaces. Aircraft were making at least five times the number of take offs and landings that they were designed to do, and engines were operating at high revs for much of their journey and only reaching normal cruising speed or altitude for relatively short periods. The wear and tear on the airframes was therefore extreme, especially on brakes, landing gear, tyres and engines. The usage of aviation fuel, specialist lubricants and consumables such as windscreen wipers increased massively, with the airlift consuming around 100 million gallons (455 million litres) of aviation fuel.

At the start of the airlift, the maintenance facilities were basic in the extreme, with poor working conditions, insufficient tools, manuals and pitiful quantities of spares. With aircraft coming from all over the world, the models and marks varied, and the maintainers found that parts were not interchangeable. This was not a problem in a small-scale squadron operation, but with a huge fleet, it became a huge issue. When trying to order parts, there were no existing consumption rates as nothing like this had ever been done before – the supply clerks had nothing to go on, so they made it up as they went along. Planned maintenance after a certain number of hours flown came around after only a few days of operation, throwing the workshops into chaos.

The maintenance situation was less of an issue for the RAF, as their home bases were just a short hop over the Channel, with RAF Abingdon, Lyneham, Dishforth and Honington all undertaking overhauls and repair work. Civilian operations such as Marshalls, Field Aircraft Services, Scottish Aviation and Airwork Ltd also provided maintenance services, as well as providing contract aircraft in some cases. However, the USAF faced monumental problems. The teams quickly adapted, with daily parts express trains being organised between their maintenance depots at Erding and Oberpfaffenhofen in southern Germany and the active airlift bases of Rhine-Main and Wiesbaden.[28] The decision was made to re-activate the wartime US maintenance depot at Burtonwood in Cheshire, England, which could handle deep maintenance requirements, and this went operational on 5 November 1948. The planners also organised a consolidated daily requirements list for the regular parts shipments coming from the US, which were ferried over by aircraft or by ship, using the Marinex high-speed ocean shipping service.

In order to keep the required number of operational aircraft in the air, there would be a similar, if not greater number of aircraft being worked on by the various maintenance teams. For example, at the peak of the airlift, to keep the optimum figure of 128 US aircraft flying, there would be an additional 196 aircraft somewhere in the system, as detailed in Table 7.

The vehicles used to transport goods from the railheads to the aircraft and move people and equipment around the bases also suffered similar excessive wear and tear problems as the aircraft, as did the radio and radar equipment. Shortages of spare parts and insufficient trained personnel were constant problems.

It was not just the aircraft and vehicles that suffered from wear and tear: the pilots, aircrew, ground crew and support staff worked incredibly long hours under very difficult and stressful conditions. In the early days of the airlift, facilities were very basic, with personnel living and working in temporary accommodation in tents, hangers and any structures available in the vicinity of the base. There were not enough beds to go around, so personnel had to sleep in shifts. Such discomfort and exhaustion could be tolerated for a short period, especially by the military, but over a longer period it impacted on morale, efficiency and degraded individuals' overall performance. In as complex and dangerous operation as the airlift certainly was, where lives depended on other people doing their job properly, such deterioration of performance was a serious issue. Slowly but surely, the

Table 7: Snapshot of USAF Aircraft Undergoing Maintenance (USAFE, Berlin Airlift)		
324	**Aircraft allocated by USAF to Airlift and Support**	
66	Aircraft with contractors for 1,000-hour inspections	USA
21	Aircraft held in pool at San Antonio and Moffett AFBs	USA
12	Aircraft being ferried to European theatre	In Transit
33	Aircraft at Burtonwood (200-hour inspections)	UK
16	Aircraft in Base repair shops	Germany
5	Aircraft in 1st and 3rd Intermediate Inspection (50 and 150 hours)	Germany
6	Aircraft in 2nd Intermediate Inspection (100 hours)	Germany
37	Aircraft in unscheduled maintenance	Germany
196	Aircraft in maintenance	Various
128	**Aircraft in commission flying the Airlift**	**Germany**

personnel infrastructure at the various operating bases in the British and American Zones of Germany and the western sectors of Berlin began to improve and resemble proper military establishments; with mess halls, laundries, snack bars, cinemas and recreational facilities such as the British NAAFI and the American PX operations. Housing quality slowly improved as well. The 24-hour airlift operation meant that these support functions also had to operate all hours of the day and night to serve the personnel as they came and went.

As the airlift developed, American personnel started to be based at British bases, sometimes under the command of British officers, and sometimes under their own. What quickly became evident was the different standards of accommodation and facilities expected by the men. For example, when Americans arrived at Faßberg, they found the British facilities primitive and vigorously complained to higher authority until they were improved. Rations were also pooled, which again caused much consternation from the Americans. The standard US Field Ration 'A' consisted of about 3,600 calories worth of food, but British rations only provided 2,600, along with strange delicacies such as tinned herrings and copious amounts of tea (as opposed to coffee), alien to the US palate. An acceptable solution was found by shipping in extra 'A' Rations allowing all military personnel, both British and American, to enjoy the better American food, while the meagre British fare was foisted off to the German civilian workers, who proved to be less fussy.

With so many crews and aircraft employed in the airlift, the RAF were forced to put much of their multi-engine and transport aircrew training on hold. This also negatively impacted Bomber Command, Army Cooperation training and even parachute training. As the airlift progressed, other parts of the RAF began to grind to a halt, so eventually they reluctantly had to pull a number of experienced crews and aircraft from the operation so that training could recommence. They also had to stop demobilising mechanics because of skill shortages, and before long, other trades such as clerks, drivers and cooks were kept on beyond their expected tours. British aircrew had the advantage of regular trips back across the Channel as aircraft were rotated back for maintenance, helping to break up the monotony.

The pace of operations was so intense that pilots and aircrew began to show signs of 'battle fatigue', exhibiting signs of exhaustion, poor morale and even disciplinary problems. Tours had been extended and extended again because of a lack of pilots, and the poor living conditions further degraded performance. By October, the USAF had to recall some 10,000 aircrew, mechanics and key support staff to duty to attempt to relieve the pressure. The demand for pilots was so high that the USAF set up a Replacement Training Unit (RTU) at Great Falls, Montana, with a full-scale mock-up of the airfields, beacons, radio frequencies, glide paths and runways that a crew would experience on the Berlin run, flying around with 8-ton loads of sand in their aircraft. They also had to be specially trained to cope with the challenging weather conditions that central Europe often experienced. The first graduates of this programme began arriving in November 1948 and provided a steady flow of replacement aircrew from then on.

The USAF responded to the problems of having personnel away from their families for extended periods by trying to improve living conditions, running an education programme to make sure everyone knew the reason for their presence in Germany at that time, improving recreational facilities and entertainment and even setting up radio links to allow airmen to speak to their families living on bases all around the globe. The US European Command created recreation areas in the Bavarian Alps for airlift personnel, requisitioning top class hotels and arranging transport. Bob Hope was booked for a tour over Christmas 1948 at Wiesbaden, Tempelhof, Faßberg and Celle. Accompanied by

song writing legend Irving Berlin, Hope teased him that with a name like that, he risked being divided into four sectors.[29] The Tempelhof show was recorded and broadcast all over the US, further raising the profile of the airlift among the American public.

A key lesson learnt during the airlift was the impact of unit cohesion on morale, especially in the RAF, where everything revolved around the individual squadron. Initially a pool of ground crew was made up of personnel wherever they could be found, so there was a real mix of trades from all over the service, however, these crews struggled with gelling together as an effective organisation. By the end of the year, the RAF reorganised personnel along squadron lines, and saw a big jump in efficiency and morale.

Local labour had been limited to loading and unloading but towards the end of the year, German mechanics began to be recruited. A former Luftwaffe general helped run the programme and arrange training and for maintenance manuals to be translated into German. The programme helped fill gaps in manning that could have quickly grounded aircraft, although the Germans were supervised closely and only given limited responsibility.

Morale amongst airlift personnel was measured by monitoring AWOL (Absence Without Leave) rates and cases of Venereal Disease (VD). The assumption that both would be higher if morale was low. US VD rates at Celle and Faßberg were particularly high, as they were forced to endure British style accommodation and recreational facilities. However, to quote the official USAFE report, 'The British cooperated whole-heartedly in picking up loose German women for necessary medical examination and confinement when required'.

Tunner succeeded Smith at the end of July 1948 and began tackling the operation with ruthless efficiency. The first order he received from his superior, Commanding General USAFE General LeMay, included '... the mission of the Airlift Task Force (Provisional) is to provide airlift to Berlin and other places as directed by the Commanding General, USAFE ...' Using techniques from the world of big business, the automotive sector in particular, his team analysed every aspect of the operation in minute detail using time and motion study techniques, eliminating wastage, duplication and inefficiency. Aircrew flying under Tunner, were cogs in a very well-oiled machine, and while the flying lacked the glamour of fighter operations and there was no room for individuality. Aircrew would have hopefully got some satisfaction from the precision of the mission and delivery of much material to a desperate city. Tunner demanded '... a steady even rhythm with hundreds of airplanes doing exactly the same thing every hour, day and night, at the same persistent beat' and his team came up with a number of key innovations and initiatives both in the air and on the ground, all of which added to the potential tonnage.

Once landed, aircrew would typically head off in search of food and drink, their next tasking or a weather briefing and often were nowhere to be seen when the unloaders/loaders had finished, wasting precious minutes on the ground. It was also dangerous having so many people wandering around an extremely busy airfield apron. Tunner therefore ordered the aircrew to remain with their aircraft while they were being unloaded, sending out mobile snack bars, briefing vehicles and operations staff in jeeps to the aircraft. He even insisted the aircrew exit the aircraft through the cockpit crew hatch – rather than via the cargo doors – so that the crew did not get in the way of the unloaders/loaders.

Tunner did not want valuable cargo carrying capacity waiting around in Berlin to be loaded with outward bound freight, so he limited that to the smaller and slower C-47s, allowing the bigger and faster C-54s to focus on bulk inbound cargos. He also diverted almost all of the passenger traffic, especially the outbound refugee traffic, to the RAF. All unnecessary equipment was to be stripped from the aircraft to save weight, including oxygen systems (the aircraft would not be going above 10,000ft (3,048m) where oxygen was needed) and redundant military and communications equipment. The resulting saving could be as much as a ton, allowing that weight to be replaced by precious cargo. The all-up-weight of the aircraft could also be reduced by only filling up with the fuel needed for the actual journey, rather than filling up the tanks to the top.

Crucially, Tunner ended the system of 'stacking' aircraft waiting to land in bad weather or if there was a delay on the ground. If an aircraft missed its landing slot, for whatever reason, it had to return to base along the central corridor and start again. From this efficiency drive, Tunner was able to increase the aircraft utilisation rates from an average of 5 ½ hours a day in July 1948 to an average of 9 ½ hours a day in April 1949.

Planners also looked at the wider organisation, looking for improvements from the very top to the bottom. Very early on, they realised that the supply and demand planning that kept the airlift going needed better coordination to avoid duplication and conflicting priorities so in mid-July 1948 they created an Airlift Staff Committee in Berlin with representatives of all three Allied powers, who would liaise with their counterparts in western Germany. On 15 October 1948, the USAFE and BAFO created a unified command structure with the creation of the Combined Airlift Task Force (CALTF), headed by Tunner. Its brief was very simple: 'To effect delivery to Berlin, in a safe and efficient manner, the maximum tonnage possible, consistent with the combined resources of equipment and personnel made available …'[30]

This new organisation was dominated by US personnel and was a 'joint' operation in name only, but it did streamline operations and smooth out traffic flow along the corridors. The decision was also made to consolidate a particular aircraft type to a particular supply base, and even consolidating particular types of freight to a particular base and/ or aircraft, all of which made loading/unloading, route planning and maintenance much easier. Different aircraft took different times to load or unload and flew at different speeds, so specialising in one particular aircraft improved efficiency and tons delivered, experimenting with various combinations before they found the ideal mix. This resulted in American aircraft being located on British bases, allowing Tunner to use his big aircraft on the shorter northern corridors, thus maximising the potential tonnage. Also, by spreading the C-54s over several bases both in the US and the British Zones, despite having to duplicate support functions, it meant that not all aircraft would be grounded by localised bad weather. While the mainstay of the operation was the C-47 and then the C-54, Tunner also experimented with several larger aircraft, such as the C-74 and C-82, with mixed results.

There was a potential downside to this specialisation, as large numbers of a particular air asset were located in one place at a particular time. Should the confrontation in Berlin turn into a shooting war, then these concentrations of aircraft would have made very tempting targets for the Soviets. However, expediency ruled the day and Tunner was given a remarkably free rein to get on with the job.

By the start of 1949, the organisation was running like a well-oiled machine. The system worked as follows:

- By the 25th of each month, CALTF's traffic section prepared a forecast of their tonnage capacity for the following month, factoring in the expected number of available aircraft, planned maintenance and the weather.
- The Air Staff Committee in Berlin would pull together a 'shopping list' which consolidated the needs of the city as fed

in by the Senat and the garrisons, setting the next month's priorities.
- This would be passed to the Berlin Airlift Committee (BEALCOM) in Frankfurt, who would allocate tonnages of specific items to their various customers; the Bipartite Control Office (BICO, part of the German Bizonal Economic Council), the British, American and French militaries and the airlift transport organisation servicing the British and American airbases in western Germany and on to Berlin.[31]
- The British Army (RASC) and US Army (Airlift Support Command) would then take delivery of the goods, moving them planeside to be loaded onto aircraft using local German labour, which would then be flown to one of the three Berlin airfields for onward distribution.

With adversity comes invention, and there were a number of small innovations that had a big impact on the airlift operation, from finding a way of reconditioning spark plugs for engines, which were in short supply, to using a spare jet engine mounted on a truck for de-icing aircraft, to converting buses to provide warm and dry shelters for aircrew close to their aircraft. To help build the new runway at Tegel, someone found a way of carefully cutting up huge earth moving and construction equipment using an oxy acetylene torch. The smaller pieces could then fit into the back of one of the rear loading Fairchild C-82 Packet aircraft, which were flown into the city and welded back together, speeding the completion of the runway.

The airlift operations went a long way to standardise procedures and protocols between the different services and between nations and this interoperability became a key aspect of NATO, which was created while the airlift was going on.[32]

The Soviet Response

The Soviet's only real answer to the airlift would have been to shoot down the Allied aircraft traversing their territory along the air corridor, but that would have almost certainly led to war. In fact, most of the troops defending the western sectors and their airfields were convinced that the Soviets would respond militarily prompting the start of a Third World War – it was only a matter of time.

The Soviets blustered a lot, but actually did very little, which was a great surprise for the Allies, who expected regular disruption of electricity supply, aggressive manoeuvres or even attacks on aircraft, more attempts to jam radio traffic, the placing of dummy navigation beacons in order to lure aircraft out of the corridors and the positioning of barrage balloons along the routes.

The British and Americans were genuinely surprised with how little the Soviets actually interfered with the airlift, limiting their displeasure to sporadic incidents of aggressive flying. The Soviets did appear to enjoy 'playing chicken' with Allied pilots by performing high-speed passes straight towards the much slower transport aircraft and seeing who would 'flinch' first. Before the airlift started, such a 'game' ended in a mid-air collision, killing the pilot and all crew and passengers in the Allied aircraft.[33]

However, while the Soviets did not appear to be prepared to use force to ensure their blockade, they were not going to leave it all to the Western Allies and they intensified their programme of harassment. Within the Soviet Zone of Occupation (what would become East Germany) large scale military exercises were conducted on the ground and in the air, sometimes 'accidentally' straying into the air corridors. Anti-aircraft batteries were positioned threateningly under the flight paths and fighters and batteries conducted live firing exercises close to where the transports were flying. Some of the tactics used were sophisticated, such as the electronic jamming of Allied radio frequencies while others were brutally simple, such as trying to dazzle the pilots with powerful searchlights as they came into land. Both the BAFO and USAFE developed rudimentary electronic countermeasures in case the Soviets began actively jamming.

The harassment of members of the Western occupying forces was not just restricted to the air. Allied officers living off base would get threatening or silent phone calls and the doorbell would be rung in the middle of the night, only to find no-one there. This only had the effect of interrupting sleep and fraying the nerves but would certainly have had a cumulatively negative impact on the officers and their families. More sinister, however, was the communist infiltration of local government and the police.

SED mob storming City Hall, 6 September 1948. (US Army Military History Institute)

Following their pattern across all of local government, the Soviets had appointed a former Nazi turned communist called Paul Markgraf as Chief of Police at the central Berlin police station in the Soviet sector. He quickly began expelling non-communists with a view to having an all-communist force. On 26 July 1948, at the height of the blockade, the city government, the Magistrat, suspended him for his continued insubordination and replaced him with Dr Johannes Stumm, an SPD appointee.[34] The Soviets refused to recognise Markgraf's suspension, so the Magistrat was forced to make a call on the future of Berlin's policing. Stumm set up an alternative police headquarters in the American sector and ordered all Berlin's police to report there. Some 1,500 of the 2,000 strong force chose to make the move, leaving Markgraf, for the time being, with a much smaller force in the Soviet sector. The police department was the first of the city's departments to split. The Soviet authorities took exception to this new organisation and any West Berlin police officer straying into the Soviet sector could expect to be beaten up or arrested.

A similar split occurred in the Central Food Office after the Soviets directly intervened in its running. As a result, on 10 August, the department had to relocate to West Berlin to continue its important work. The Finance Department would also split in November, quickly followed by most of the other functions in City Hall. Thousands of undesirable (that is, non-communist) city workers were sacked in the months leading to the final split of local government.

The Berlin civilian local government was based out of the Rotes Rathaus (Red City Hall), an imposing red brick building in Mitte district, near Alexanderplatz in the Soviet sector. Beginning in June, the Soviets decided to start disrupting the assembly meetings by sending in 'rent-a-mobs' of SED supporters to intimidate the members, wreck the proceedings and try to force the non-communist councillors out.[35] On 6 September 1948, this intervention took a more sinister turn when a large communist crowd protected by Soviet sector police officers stormed the chamber and occupied most of the building.

The councillors (known as Senators) had to flee for their lives, many escaping to the British sector, but a number of the western sector police who were guarding the building were arrested and detained in the Soviet sector. They were held for over a month until pressure from the UN secured their release.

On 9 September 1948, a huge crowd gathered at the Platz der Republik in front of the old Reichstag building, just along from the Brandenburg Gate and right next to the sector border between the British and Soviet sectors.[36] The crowd was protesting about the blockade and Soviet intimidation and quickly grew to over 300,000 strong, the biggest democratic demonstration in Berlin's political history. Speaker after speaker criticised the Soviets and the communist authorities before being addressed by Ernst Reuter, the elected Berlin Mayor, called on the international community not to abandon his city:[37] 'People of the world! People in America, in England, in France, in Italy! Look upon this city and see that you should not – you cannot – abandon this city and its people.'[38]

This famous speech ranks alongside Kennedy's 'Ich bin ein Berliner' speech of 1963 and Reagan's 'Mr. Gorbachev, tear down this wall!' speech of 1987 as key moments of drama in Berlin's Cold War history. As the demonstration began to break up, elements within the crowd confronted Soviet troops who were nearby, guarding the Soviet War Memorial and the sector border. British troops succeeded in breaking up much of the crowd, but some began stoning the Soviet troops and a group managed to climb the Brandenburg Gate, ripping down the Soviet flag that had flown there since 1945. That was the final straw for the Soviets, who opened fire on the crowd, killing a 15-year-old Berliner and proceeded to violently break up the demonstrators, making several arrests. Around 25 others were seriously injured, and five Berliners were subsequently imprisoned for 25 years for 'Assault on the Occupation Forces' and 'Injuries to Public Order'. The Soviets decided to make an example of these youths to deter further demonstrations against the communist authorities.

The attempted communist take-over of the police and the local government furthered the divide between the Western and Soviet sectors. The Magistrat gave up holding meetings at the Rotes Rathaus and moved as the Senat to the Rathaus Schöneberg (Schöneberg Town Hall) in the Tempelhof-Schöneberg Borough of the American Sector, where they would remain until reunification. The Eastern Sector assembly would go on to 'elect' their own Lord Mayor of Berlin, Friedrich Ebert Jr., who was instantly recognised by the Soviets, and who would argue that his assembly was the only 'legal' administration in the city. The election held in the three western zones in December 1948 drove the final wedge between the two rival local government organisations in the city. The communists openly questioned the validity of the election and urged voters not to turn up or to spoil their ballot papers. They also threatened to disrupt the actual voting. As it happened, there was little disruption and a massive turnout gave the SPD a substantial majority, with very few spoilt papers. The citizens of West Berlin had overwhelmingly

US Skymaster C-54 flies low over people on approach to land at Tempelhof. (US Army Military History Institute)

rejected the calls from the Soviets and their German puppets and Berlin was effectively a divided city from then on.

The traffic was not just a one-way flow of food, fuel and general day-to-day necessities into West Berlin, and the planners tried to ensure that the aircraft did not return empty. There was a difference of opinion between the British and Americans about these return legs. The efficiency-orientated Americans wanted to send the aircraft back on its way as soon as it had been unloaded, to allow it to make the next round trip. The British, however, recognised the humanitarian and economic justifications for sending the aircraft back loaded to the brim. They took the opportunity to evacuate thousands of half-starving orphaned street children and the sick and elderly into the care of the hospitals in the West. The Americans did however transport over 60,000 mostly military and administrative staff in and out of Berlin. A daily passenger flight from Wiesbaden to Berlin carried a total of 19,000 French passengers inbound and outbound.

Table 8: Passenger Operations[39]

	Inbound	Outbound	Total
US	25,263	37,486	62,749
UK	34,815	130,091	164,906
Total	60,078	167,577	227,655

CALTF also saw the strategic value of providing a transport service for West Berlin's recovering industry – if businesses could not operate, then it would cause more unemployment and long-term problems for the city. When it did not interfere with schedules, the returning aircraft were loaded up with goods produced in West Berlin's factories to be distributed to markets in West Germany and beyond. In the first 5 months of 1949, goods to the value of $6 million were exported. Goods

were marked 'Hergestellt im Blockierten Berlin' – 'Manufactured in Blockaded Berlin'!

Table 9: Outbound Cargo

Country	Tonnage
US	45,888
UK	35,843
Total	81,731

Both sides were quick to try to exploit the operation for propaganda purposes. Within a few days of the start of the blockade, Berlin was saturated with Soviet controlled newspapers spreading negative propaganda about the airlift and telling the civilian population that the efforts were a token but futile gesture, and merely a prelude to the West abandoning the city.

In response, the Allied powers began their own positive propaganda campaign. They prioritised the delivery of newsprint to print newspapers over many other essential items, so an alternative message could be delivered to the worried citizens in the western sectors. As early as the end of June 1948, German reporters, photographers and commentators were permitted to fly on airlift aircraft in order to report back to the citizens of Berlin and the western sectors of Occupied Germany on the unprecedented effort underway. The news was just as important for the other European countries as well as the US domestic audience, especially as the North Atlantic Alliance was finally coming together. Tunner's tonnage blitz events, such as the USAF 1st birthday push in September 1948 and the 'Easter Parade' in April 1949 made headlines all over the world. Also, the news in August 1948 that the airlift had exceeded its daily tonnage target (4,742 vs. 4,500) for the first time and in April 1949, when Tunner announced they were bringing in more by air than they had been by road and rail, were genuine achievements and therefore key news events that won support in London and Washington while giving Stalin a serious problem.

In the city, the Allies tried to deliver a few small rays of sunshine in the Berliner's grim day-to-day existence and of course made sure it got covered in the press. For example, they hosted parties giving the children of Berlin, who had grown up during the war, their first taste of sweets and chocolate. Concerts were popular with the Berliners as well as with servicemen stationed in the city.

The most famous 'hearts and minds' episode was Operation Little Vittles by the Rosinenbomber (Raisin Bomber, Candy Bomber or Chocolate Flyer). On a trip into the city, USAF pilot Lieutenant Gail S Halvorsen witnessed the tough conditions the Berliners were living in and decided to drop a bit of happiness over the city next time he was flying in. He wrapped up some sweets and gum in handkerchiefs and got his crew chief to drop them out of the aircraft as he was making his approach to land. Word got around and soon there were crowds of children waiting at the beginning of the runway. Halvorsen and his colleagues cleared the PX at Rhein-Main and Wiesbaden airbases out of sweets and chocolate and scavenged sheets, old shirts and every spare piece of fabric they could find to make the tiny parachute packages which were dropped to the excited children.[40]

The press soon became aware of the story and donations began flooding in from the States. This goodwill operation soon grew so big that it became a dangerous distraction for aircrews, and the top brass intervened, bringing the 'Raisin Bombers' to an end. The packages kept coming but were delivered in bulk into the city for onward distribution. The citizens of what would become West Germany also joined in with the goodwill parcels, contributing practical items such as candles, seedlings, coal and food, as well as giving direct financial support. All this outpouring of international goodwill infuriated the Soviets, who hated seeing the Westerners club together to save the city.

The Allied governments met in London in July 1948 to come up with a strategic response to the crisis. Frank Roberts, then Private Secretary to British Foreign Secretary Ernest Bevin, was despatched to Moscow to see if a solution could be reached.[41] Over the period of two weeks, Roberts met with Molotov and twice with Stalin, but the meetings ended without agreement – the Soviets would not budge on any of Roberts' suggestions. In September, the Allies lodged a formal complaint with the UN, stating that the Soviets' 'illegal' blockade was a threat to international peace and security.

Faced with a diplomatic deadlock, the city hunkered down for a long siege and began to stockpile any surplus food and fuel. With priority being given on coal deliveries to industry and hospital, Berlin was systematically stripped of all combustible material to use for domestic heating, including uprooting what was left of their precious Tiergarten. Shops in the East were well stocked, and with the sector borders still notionally open, West Berlin housewives crossed over to try to buy fresh fruit and vegetables, although they risked harassment by the Volkspolizei and the confiscation of their purchases. The Soviets and the new East German authorities tried to lure West Berliners over to live, with the promise of generous ration cards and bountiful supplies, but very few (less than 20,000 in total) took up the offer. It would only be a few years before the situation was dramatically reversed, and with no opportunities for free movement.

In the early days of the airlift when goods were still on the shelves and factories and businesses were still operating, the West Berliners paid little interest to the squabbling occupation powers, but as the blockade dragged on, it started to become an obsession for many citizens, closely monitoring the daily tonnage statistics reported in the press. The drone of low flying aircraft soon became part of the city's soundscape, to the extent that any gaps in the flying, perhaps as the result of bad weather, were instantly noticed by the worried West Berliners.

There was no doubt that life was tough for Berliners during the blockade and they had to endure shortages of staple foods and fuel for heating. Coal was prioritised for electricity production and heating hospitals so there was very little left for domestic heating or for schools and workplaces. The diet was monotonous and was barely above subsistence levels, although small vegetable plots appeared on available ground until the frosts came along. Remarkably, West Berlin's population stayed reasonably healthy, with many of the sick and elderly being evacuated on the return leg to West Germany. With the electricity supply only running for a few hours a day, businesses struggled to operate, with unemployment tripling while the blockade was in place. The Magistrat responded with civic work projects, which at least started to clear some of the rubble around the embattled city. The citizens of Berlin were a resilient bunch who maintained their particular sense of humour through some very difficult times.

The programmes on Berlin Radio (Berliner Rundfunk), the radio station controlled by the Soviets, poured out endless negative propaganda about the airlift and how it was failing, and that the British and Americans were about to pull out of the city. Back in February 1946, realising that the Soviets were not going to relinquish control of Berlin Radio, the Americans began broadcasting RIAS, or Radio In (the) American Sector and its powerful transmitters gave the people of Berlin, both West and East, an alternative mix of news, panel discussions, music, entertainment and comedy, providing much needed light relief from the daily grind and the heavily biased and stuffy content provided by the Soviets. Humour played a big role in Berliners' lives and the German language presenters and actors on RIAS would openly mock the Soviets, much to their annoyance. One classic sketch concerned the coming Christmas period, and the comedian told his audience that no expense was being spared to ensure that Berliners were going to have a good Christmas – the Americans were going to fly in powdered Christmas trees that could be reconstituted with water![42]

To try to drown out the Berliner Rundfunk transmissions, the Allies began a 'transmitter race' with the Soviets. RIAS's first transmitter had a 1000w output, which was increased to 2,500w in early 1947 in response to Soviet improvements. By July 1947, they had installed a massive 20,000w transmitter with a 47-mile (75km) radius and by the time of the airlift, their transmitter had grown to 100,000w, reaching a listening public of around 40 million people. During the blockade, the station began broadcasting 24 hours a day with all kinds of emergency public information such as the daily power allocations and ration availability. For those without receivers or electricity to power their sets, RIAS despatched mobile loudspeaker trucks around the city, so everyone was kept in the loop. The powerful transmitter also acted as a beacon for airlift pilots en route to the city.

Flying along the three narrow and crowded air corridors was a dangerous exercise and there were many accidents, both in the air and on the ground. Some were linked to Soviet harassment tactics, but most were simple flying accidents; mid-air collisions caused by overcrowded air lanes, lack of navigation aids, poor weather, inexperienced or exhausted aircrew or mechanical failure. Accidents also took place on the ground, where aircraft caught fire or collided with vehicles or people, killing military ground crew and German civilians who were employed to unload the aircraft. A few of the accidents took place over Soviet territory and they extracted every morsel of propaganda value from the individual tragedies, trying to convince the world that the airlift was not working. A total of 78 men

Table 10: Airlift Fatalities

Date	Aircraft	Tail Number	Location	Reason	Fatalities
US					
8 July 1948	C-47	43-48256	NE of Wiesbaden	Crashed into hill on approach	3 fatalities
25 July 1948	C-47	43-49534	Berlin	Crashed on final approach to Tempelhof	2 fatalities
24 August 1948	C-47	43-16036	Ravolzhausen, NE of Hanau	Mid-air collision	2 fatalities
24 August 1948	C-47	43-15116	Ravolzhausen, NE of Hanau	Mid-air collision	2 fatalities
2 October 1948	C-54	45-520	Rhein-Main	Ground accident	1 fatality
18 October 1948	C-54	42-72688	Near Rhein-Main	Hit trees on approach	3 fatalities
29 October 1948	None	N/A	Tegel	Construction accident	1 fatality
5 December 1948	C-54	42-72698	Faßberg	Crashed on take off	3 fatalities
11 December 1948	R5D	USN 5602	North of Rhein-Main	Crashed on approach	1 fatality
7 January 1949	C-54	45-5543	NE of Blackpool, England	En route to Burtonwood	6 fatalities
12 January 1949	C-54	42-72629	Near Rhein-Main	Crashed on approach	3 fatalities
18 January 1949	C-54	45-563	Faßberg	Crashed on approach	1 fatality
4 March 1949	C-54	44-9086	South corridor, east of Fulda	No. 3 engine fire	1 fatality
12 July 1949	C-54	42-72476	Rathenau, North corridor	Crashed en route from Celle to Tegel	3 fatalities
UK					
19 September 1948	York	MW288	Wunstorf	Engine failure on take off	5 fatalities
17 November 1948	Dakota	KP223	Soviet Zone, near Lübeck	Bad weather at night	4 fatalities
24 January 1949	Dakota	KN491	Soviet Zone, near Lübeck	7 German passengers also killed	1 fatality
22 March 1949	Dakota	KJ970	Lübeck		3 fatalities
16 July 1949	Hastings	TG611	Tegel	Faulty trim on take off	5 fatalities
Civilian					

Date	Aircraft and Tail No.	Company	Location	Reason	Fatalities
23 November 1948	Lancastrian G-AHJW	Flight Refuelling Ltd.	Thruxton, UK	Crash returning to UK	7 fatalities
8 December 1948	Ground accident	Airflight Ltd.	Gatow	Hit and run	1 fatality
15 January 1949	Ground accident	Lancashire Aircraft Corp	Schleswigland	Truck drove into propeller of RAF Hastings TG 521	3 fatalities
15 March 1949	York, G-AHFI	Skyways Ltd.	Gatow		3 fatalities
21 March 1949	Halton G-AJZZ	Lancashire Aircraft Corp	Schleswigland		3 fatalities
30 April 1949	Halton G-AKAC	World Air Freight	North of Tegel		4 fatalities

from Great Britain, America, Germany and other corners of the globe would lose their lives trying to keep the city of Berlin from starving, 39 British, 31 Americans and at least eight Germans.

The strain was also felt by the fighter squadrons who were tasked with protecting the air corridors. Unusual air activity by the Soviets would prompt a scramble, as would reports of a transport crashing, as it was difficult to tell whether it was because of an accident or as a result of enemy activity, possibly the start of a more substantial Soviet offensive on the city.

Looking for a way out

As 1949 began, it was clear to Stalin that his blockade was failing miserably. The success of the airlift surprised many, not least the Soviets, who were convinced the blockade would force the Western Allies to the negotiating table or even to quit the city. By August 1948, the airlift was capable of bringing in more than the minimum daily requirement – over 707 flights on 8 August brought in 4,742 tons compared to a daily requirement of 4,500 tons. By the end of the year, the 100,000th flight landed in West Berlin and by the end of February 1949, the 1,000,000th ton had been delivered (a British York loaded with potatoes).

It was a logistical triumph over serious adversity and by spring 1949, the airlift was running like a well-oiled machine. In April 1949, General Clay announced that they were bringing in more supplies by air than they would have been able to by road and rail. In fact, on 16 April 1949, the busiest day of the airlift (the 'Easter Parade'), aircraft were landing every minute, a record 1,398 flights delivering a record 12,940 tons. Every day the operation continued, the more the West were demonstrating their organisational and technical mastery over the Soviets, and they had shown that the resupply effort could continue indefinitely, if needed.

The Soviet Union's attempt to starve out the citizens of Berlin for political gain really was not looking good on the international stage and even Stalin was conscious of his image. He had also managed to alienate the German population from the Western zones, who he had been hoping to entice into a united Communist Germany, something that was clearly never going to happen.

When considering the success of the Berlin Airlift, most commentators overlook the impact that the West's counter-blockade had on the Soviet Zone and by association, the USSR. As soon as Stalin began his blockade, the Western Occupying Powers initiated a complete block on all rail and barge traffic transiting the western zones for the Soviet Zone and beyond. This freight comprised reparations as agreed at Potsdam, and regular shipments of commodities essential to the Soviet Zone's economy. Monthly deliveries of 250,000 tons of coal, 30,000 tons of steel and more than 33,000 tons of chemicals all stopped, as well as deliveries of machine tools and other industrial supplies. Heavy with irony, the Western powers blamed the breakdown of supply on 'technical difficulties', a phrase much used by the Soviets to disrupt day-to-day life in West Berlin. In September 1948, the counter-blockade was extended to include road traffic and from January 1949, they also blocked any exports from West Berlin's recovering industry from reaching the Soviet Zone.

The Soviets had not realised just how dependent industry in their zone was on trade with the Western zones. Everything from heavy industry to food production relied on regular deliveries of raw materials from the West. The Soviet Zone's industry had been comprehensively looted by NKGB reparation squads straight after the end of the war, and what was left soon ground to a halt with their deliveries being stopped at the zonal border. Extended shortages of day-to-day necessities were bound to cause civil unrest, which would undermine Ulbricht's plans for a socialist paradise. It also meant that Moscow was not able siphon off a good proportion of the shipments for use in the Soviet Union. For Stalin, the writing was on the wall and he began to look for a way out without losing face.

In January 1949, a US journalist, J. Kingsbury Smith, submitted a series of questions to Stalin, and against all expectations, Stalin replied, saying that Moscow would be prepared to lift the blockade as long as the West immediately lifted their transport and trade embargo and they delayed setting up a separate West German government until the foreign ministers from all four occupying powers could sit down to discuss Germany. Stalin had been fixated on resolving the 'German Question' since Potsdam and had hoped that his strong-arm tactics would have pushed the Allies out of the city. It certainly had not worked out like that. Remarkably, no mention was made of the status of Berlin's currency, which had been a consistent sticking point in diplomatic discussions throughout the blockade.

Thinking that this could be the start of a climb down from Moscow, an American diplomat, the deputy chief of the United States Mission to the UN in New York, Philip Jessup, was tasked with digging deeper and on 15 February asked Soviet Ambassador to the UN, Yakov Malik, whether the omission over the currency was intentional. After a month of silence, Malik came back and confirmed that the omission was indeed intentional, signalling that Stalin was prepared to start negotiating. These top secret 'back-channel' discussions were kept from the other Western Allies and even General Clay in Berlin.

Stalin had hoped that the blockade would cause rifts to form between the Western Allies, but it had the opposite effect. The US led Marshall Plan was beginning to deliver on its promise of European recovery and with prosperity, came unity. Off the back of the Marshall Plan and in response to various international crises (the blockade of Berlin being one), a number of European and North American nations came together to create an alliance based on mutual security. Negotiations over the exact terms of the alliance went back and forth during 1948 and the first few months of 1949, but by April, they had concluded.

At a ceremony in Washington DC on 4 April 1949, 12 nations came together to sign an agreement to form NATO, the North Atlantic Treaty Organization. This alliance would secure peace in post-war Europe, promote cooperation between its members and guard their freedom in face of Soviet aggression and expansionism. Belgium, Canada, Denmark, France, Iceland, Italy, Luxembourg, the Netherlands, Norway, Portugal, the United Kingdom and the United States all joined in this collective defence pact, inextricably linking the fate of the European nations with the nuclear-equipped US military.[43] Article 5 of the treaty sums this collective security up:

> The Parties agree that an armed attack against one or more of them in Europe or North America shall be considered an attack against them all…[44]

Roosevelt had told Stalin at Yalta that he planned to have all American troops home within two years of winning the war, and this would have emboldened the Soviet leader to act as he did over Berlin. However, recent events clearly demonstrated that the US now expected to have a big role in the defence of Europe for some time to come. It would also have a dramatic impact on the Soviet strategy for the blockade.

While they were in Washington, the British and French delegations met with their American counterparts to discuss Berlin. With cooperation over the Berlin Airlift and in the formation of NATO, it was inevitable that the French would eventually come into line with their fellow Western Allies, and at the end of the 'Conference of the Foreign Ministers of the Three Western Powers' in Washington DC on 8 April 1949, France was admitted to the Bizone, which therefore became a Trizone.[45] This was not a sign of renewed French cooperation, but more a legal precursor to the Trizone becoming the unified Republic of West Germany.

At the same time, the British and French were briefed on the progress of the secret back-channel talks. They accepted the concept of mutually lifting the blockades and were prepared to meet with the Soviets to discuss Germany, but with so much going on in Bonn, they were not prepared to suspend or postpone their preparations for the formation of the new West German state in order to fit around Stalin's schedule for his precious summit meeting. Faced with the success of the airlift, the formation of NATO and of the Trizone, the Soviets were not really in a position to argue. To give Malik a lifeline with Stalin (Stalin was not known for his tolerance of envoys who failed to deliver), Jessup suggested that as there was still lots to do to formalise the Federal Republic, if the Soviets acted quickly in getting the summit organised, they may well have met before the German state came into being. This may have given Stalin his way out and probably saved Malik's life.

On 4 May 1949, the parties reached an agreement at a meeting held in New York – both parties would lift their blockades on the 12 May and Stalin would get his conference on the 'German Question' on 23 May in Paris.[46]

With the three western former occupation zones now merged economically into the Trizone, all the pieces were now in place to go ahead with a full merger. On 8 May 1949, four years to the day after VE Day, the West German Parliamentary Council in Bonn adopted the 'Basic Law for the Federal Republic of Germany', allowing the British, American and French Occupation Zones together to come together to form a new democratic state: the Federal Republic of Germany (also known as the 'Bonn Republic', the FRG, 'Bundesrepublik Deutschland' or BRD).[47]

The Blockade is lifted

A minute after midnight on 12 May 1949, the power was restored to the Western Sectors of Berlin and a US Army jeep tentatively joined the autobahn heading west only to pass without any hinderance. A few minutes later, a British military vehicle passed the Soviet checkpoint at Helmstedt heading east for the city, again without interference. Soon after, the first trains and vehicle convoys bringing supplies crossed the zone borders and headed for Berlin. The blockade had been lifted after 322 days and there were major celebrations across the Western sectors of the city. In the Soviet Zone, news of the lifting of the blockade and resumption of inter-zonal trade and traffic did not even make the front page. Back in Bonn, however, the political juggernaut continued.

To all intents and purposes, the 'Basic law' was a constitution for West Germany, but the politicians shied away from actually calling it a constitution, fearing it could deepen the division of Germany into East and West. The law was intended to be of a provisional nature and would only be valid during the division until unity had been restored.[48] It was approved by the Western Allied powers on 12 May, ratified by the parliaments of more than two thirds of the participating German Länder in the week of 16 to 22 May and the Federal Republic of Germany (FRG) came into being on 23 May 1949.[49] Elections for the new West German parliament, the Bundestag, took place on 14 August 1949, with Konrad Adenauer of the CDU becoming its first Chancellor.

The Washington Declaration and the Basic Law brought Military Government in West Germany to an end, transferring executive and judicial powers to the new Federal Government, putting the occupation forces into more of a supervisory position via a High Commissioner for each of the zones. This meant quite a shakeup after a very tough couple of years. Clay resigned just after the blockade was lifted in May 1949, temporarily being succeeded by Lieutenant General Clarence Huebner before handing over to John J. McCloy as the new American High Commissioner. Koenig was succeeded as French High Commissioner by André François-Poncet in September 1949, while Robertson made the transition from British Military Governor to British High Commissioner, providing much needed continuity. The occupying forces still kept the new West German government on a fairly tight leash, reserving

Ground and air crew celebrate the end of the airlift. (US Army Military History Institute)

USAF B-29s over Europe. (Albert Grandolini)

Lockheed P-80 Shooting Stars being unloaded at Glasgow docks, August 1948. (Albert Grandolini)

Germany, who had lived with an autocratic dictatorship for so many years, a stake in their own destiny was a highly symbolic and important step in Europe's post-war recovery and was all the more significant with the Soviet Union and their eastern zone not participating. This of course deepened the divide with the Soviet Union, who ruled over their eastern zone with an iron fist and the creation of the Federal Republic inadvertently cemented the future split of Germany and brought on the Cold War. Interestingly, the declaration made no mention of Berlin, which would continue to be a thorn in the former Allies' sides.

Stalin did get his summit to discuss the elusive 'German Question', beginning in Paris on 23 May 1949, which happened to be the very same day the FRG came into being, making Stalin's stipulation that the summit was to be held *before* the formation of the FRG moot. The new German state was going to be formed with or without Stalin's blessing so it may be just a coincidence that the Basic Law was ratified on that day or it may have been a very high-level dig at the Soviet leader.

Robert Schuman, French Foreign Minister, A. Y. Vyshinsky, Soviet Foreign Minister (who had replaced Molotov, sacked during the negotiations for failing to deliver on Berlin and the 'German Question'), Ernest Bevin, British Foreign Secretary and Dean Acheson, the US Secretary of State, met to discuss the future of Germany. Stalin went to great lengths to sell the meeting to his internal audience as a great victory, but after four weeks of frustrating cyclical arguments the meeting ended on 20 June 1949 with no concrete agreement.[50] The subject was bounced to the new

the right to intervene in matters of defence, reparations and foreign policy.

The creation of the FRG was the culmination of much work, starting at the EAC, at the Potsdam Conference, within the ACC and with the three Allied governments. Granting the people of West

United Nations and to further unspecified quadripartite meetings in Berlin. As all the previous quadripartite Berlin meetings had ended in acrimony and none had taken place since June 1948, this was a classic diplomatic dodge, knowing full well that for the time being, the issue was unresolvable.

Lockheed P-80 Shooting Stars being fuelled at RAF Renfrew, Glasgow, August 1948. (Albert Grandolini)

Although the blockade had been lifted, it would take months for the city to fully return to some degree of normality. The Allied Authority's planners did not want to risk a repeat of the blockade, so they continued airlift operations in order to stockpile huge quantities of food, medicine, coal, fuel and other raw materials in strategic secret locations throughout the city in order to provide a minimum of 6 months cover. In a sweet twist of fate, once the so-called Senat Reserve was disbanded in 1990, the 90,000 tons of supplies were donated to the Soviet Union!

As quickly as it had begun, the airlift operation wound down. The phase out began on the 1 August with some units being sent home and the first of the airfields was closed down. The British terminated the use of civilian contract flights on 16 August 1949. The military task force went to a five-day week, then to daytime operations only and the tonnage dropped right off. CALTF was disbanded on 1 September and one by one the different cogs in General Tunner's well-oiled machine were disassembled and sent back to the US, across the Channel to Great Britain or relocated to an enlarged British and American presence in West Germany.

The final American flight of the airlift took place on 30 September 1949, with a C-54 delivering two and a half tons of coal. The last British flight was 6 October, a total of 470 days after the blockade began. The US Airlift Task Force disbanded at one minute past midnight on 1 October 1949, while 46 Group RAF returned to the UK on 15 October. The Soviets showed no sign of resuming the blockade, so the reserve forces kept in West Germany were soon stood down and by the end of the year, the great endeavour called the Berlin Airlift finally came to an end.

In total, 2,325,654 tons of supplies were airlifted into Berlin between June 1948 and September 1949, 1,783,573 by the Americans and 542,081 by the British. Of the 277,682 flights made, 189,963 were by the Americans and 87,719 by the British. Some 124,000,000 miles (200,000,000km) were flown, equivalent to 520 trips to the moon or almost 5,000 times around the world. 167,577 people were flown out of Berlin on the return leg of the flights (mostly by the British) and 81,731 tons of exports from Berlin manufacturers were shipped out

of the city. The airlift cost the Americans $350 million (also quoted at $224 million), the British £17 million and the West Germans DM150 million.

The 1948-49 Berlin crisis can be credited with creating a geopolitical legacy in the United Kingdom, that lasted throughout the Cold War and beyond. As the tension grew over Stalin's intentions for the city, the Americans decided in a very public and provocative way to position their B-29 bombers, the aircraft that dropped the bombs on Hiroshima and Nagasaki, on British soil. In the years following the end of the war, the momentum of nuclear weapons development faltered as part of the so-called peace dividend, but as relations with their former ally soured, US President Truman authorised an accelerated programme of testing, development and stockpiling. At the same time, the Pentagon and State Department lobbied Truman for clarification on what circumstances would prompt use of atomic weapons in a crisis such as the one experienced by Berlin. In 1947, the US possessed only 13 bombs, but by 1948, this had grown to 50, and to one hundred and seventy in 1949.[51] The stockpile continued to increase exponentially through to the late 1960s.[52] While the 50 weapons in 1948 could do a lot of damage, they were still fairly thin on the ground, but despite the KGB's best efforts, Stalin did not know the size of America's stockpile, assuming it was much bigger. Even if the use of atomic weapons was discounted, the B-29s and the RAF Lincoln heavy bombers could deliver a massive conventional bomb load right onto the Kremlin. The positioning of the US's strategic bomber force within striking distance of Moscow sent a very strong message to Stalin that the US possessed the means to decisively counter any military aggression over Berlin.

The siting of the B-29s in Britain was permitted under an informal agreement between the British and American governments. In July 1948, the Air Ministry announced that two B-29 bomber groups (about 60 aircraft) would be based 'temporarily' in the UK as part of a normal long-range flight 'training' programme.

The posting was initially for 30 days, which got extended to 60, then to 90 before becoming a permanent fixture. Bases were established at RAF Waddington in Lincolnshire and RAF Marham in Norfolk and some 1,500 personnel were deployed including ground and aircrews. Within a few weeks, more bombers had arrived at RAF Scampton in Lincolnshire and RAF Lakenheath in Suffolk and in early 1949 also at RAF Sculthorpe in Norfolk. The B-29 also made use of the supply and maintenance depot at RAF Burtonwood in Cheshire. In September 1948, British Prime Minister Clement Attlee agreed to the American request for permission to assemble American atomic weapons on British soil and, in the event of war, for nuclear armed aircraft to take off from British airfields.

The bombers were accompanied with swarms of the latest jet fighters, which would be based in Germany. Eighty-two Lockheed P-80 Shooting Stars of the 36th Fighter Bomber Group departed on

The *Luftbrückendenkmal* memorial at Tempelhof Airport in Berlin. (Private Collection)

USS *Sicily* (CVE-118) on 15 July 1948, arriving in Glasgow on 7 August 1948. The aircraft were craned onto the dockside and then towed to nearby RAF Renfrew, where they were readied for flight. Between 13 and 20 August, they transited to Fürstenfeldbruck (Fursty) in West Germany, which would be their base until 1953 as part of USAFE's 12th Air Force, becoming the first US jet fighter-equipped unit in Europe.[53]

And so began a relationship between the USAF and the towns and cities of the east of England and West Germany that would last throughout the Cold War. It also ensured that if it came to war, much of the UK and West Germany would have been targeted by Soviet MRBMs and ICBMs and wiped off the face of the earth in the initial nuclear exchange between America and the Soviet Union.

There were many more practical lessons learnt, that influenced operations and strategy as the Cold War intensified. Apart from its obvious humanitarian value, the airlift provided extremely valuable experience for long and short haul transport operations, and this would pay dividends when the Korean War began in 1950, and later in Vietnam. It also gave the British and Americans (and to a lesser extent, the French) invaluable experience of post-war multi-national combined operations. It demonstrated the importance of a clear

command structure when operating in such an organisation, which was especially important following the formation of NATO. The airlift severely tested the interoperability between different nations and between different arms of the military within nations, highlighting the need for standardisation of equipment, procedures and units of measure. Both militaries recognised the value of unit/squadron integrity for long-term morale and efficiency.

On a more prosaic level, the operation demonstrated the immense importance of radar and other air traffic control techniques, with airlift innovations benefiting military and civilian aviation for years to come. There were big lessons learnt for future aircraft design, with the trend for positioning loading access either at the front or the rear, rather than through side door. For example, the ubiquitous Lockheed C-130 Hercules, which entered service in 1956, benefited from this experience, as have all other military transports since.

The civilian contractors, despite their unconventional approach, proved to be a hugely valuable part of the operation and pioneered the collaboration between civilians and military that we see in today's armed forces. The operation also debuted the application of scientific and commercial techniques to military problems, which US Secretary of Defense Robert McNamara took to new heights during the Vietnam War. It also demonstrated the value of adopting an attitude of flexible continuous improvement, as preached by General Tunner, showing that small ideas can yield big benefits.

In 1951, the city of Berlin erected a memorial at Tempelhof Airport, the *Luftbrückendenkmal*, which is supposed to represent three arcs pointing towards the west, symbolising the three air corridors. The Berliners call it the *Hungerkralle* (hunger claw) or *Hungerharke* (hunger rake). Further memorials were erected at Frankfurt am Main in 1985 and Celle in 1988. In 1959, on the 10th anniversary of the end of the blockade, Berlin Mayor (and future German Chancellor) Willy Brandt set up the Airlift Gratitude Foundation (*Die Stiftung Luftbrückendank*) to express Berlin's gratitude to the countries that carried out the operation and to provide financial support to the families of the 78 men who lost their lives in the air and on the ground. The airlift created a special bond between the citizens of Berlin and the Allied garrisons, which endured throughout the Cold War.

CONCLUSION

Stalin may have lifted his blockade of Berlin on 12 May 1949, but events in the remaining months of the decade would ensure that the post-war uncertainties and danger would continue into the 1950s. On 29 August 1949, at the Semipalatinsk Test Site in Kazakhstan, the Soviet Union successfully tested their first atomic device, which they codenamed RDS-1 or First Lightning. The US called it JOE-1 after its patron, Joseph Stalin. The weapon was a near copy of Fat Man, the bomb dropped on Nagasaki, using the detailed design descriptions provided by British traitor Klaus Fuchs, and had a similar yield of 22 kilotons. US monitoring stations picked up unusual seismic activity coming from the Soviet Union, and 'sniffer' aircraft picked up radioactive air samples confirming the news that the Soviets had tested an atomic bomb. In a sombre address on 23 September, Truman broke the news to the US public, calling for international control of these weapons, while privately pushing for the expansion of the US atomic arsenal and the development of the hydrogen bomb. The world had entered a very dangerous phase.

On 1 October 1949, after a long and bloody civil war, Mao Zedong declared the founding of the People's Republic of China (PRC) under his Chinese Communist Party (CPC). The pro-West leader of the Nationalist Party, or Kuomintang (KMT), Generalissimo Chiang Kai-shek, was forced into exile on the island of Taiwan (formerly Formosa), creating the confusingly titled Republic of China (ROC).[1] The world now had a second communist state, which threatened peace and stability in the Far East. Truman would go on to be criticised for allowing China to be lost to communism and the world would not have to wait for long before Chairman Mao began to flex his muscles.

The situation in Berlin and Germany also became much more complicated as both sides entrenched their respective positions. The western occupation zones (the British, French and American) had merged into the Trizone, which became the Federal Republic of Germany (that is, West Germany) on 23 May 1949, while the airlift was still underway. Ulbricht managed to get his way and on 7 October 1949, a new State was created from the Soviet Occupation Zone –

the Deutsche Demokratische Republik (DDR, German Democratic Republic, GDR or East Germany) was formed, notionally ruled by the SED, but really controlled by Stalin. Germany had been split politically right down the middle, and Berlin, its former capital and located deep within the DDR, was in the bizarre situation of being split between the four occupying powers into four sectors. For the moment, the divide was just political, but that would soon change.

The Berlin blockade and airlift was the first major confrontation of the new Cold War and had ended in a humiliating climb down by Stalin, making the formal division of the city a certainty. Of all of the world leaders, Stalin was prepared to play the long game and would continue to keep squeezing the capitalist enclave of West Berlin for many years to come, ensuring that Berlin would remain right on the Cold War front line.

Appendix 1: The Airlift in Numbers

Tonnage Delivered[1]							
	US	British	Total	US	British	Total	Tons per
	Tonnage	Tonnage	Tonnage	Flights	Flights*	Flights	Flight
June 1948	1,199	347	1,546	474	139	613	2.5
July 1948	39,971	29,035	69,006	7,550	5,978	13,528	5.1
August 1948	73,658	45,345	119,003	9,770	8,372	18,142	6.6
September 1948	101,847	37,776	139,623	12,904	6,825	19,729	7.1
October 1948	115,793	31,789	147,582	12,135	6,100	18,235	8.1
November 1948	87,979	25,609	113,588	9,047	4,305	13,352	8.5
December 1948	114,567	26,871	141,438	11,660	4,832	16,492	8.6
January 1949	139,219	32,740	171,959	14,095	5,397	19,492	8.8
February 1949	120,395	31,846	152,241	12,043	5,043	17,086	8.9
March 1949	154,475	41,686	196,161	15,530	6,633	22,163	8.9
April 1949	189,957	45,407	235,364	19,130	6,896	26,026	9.0
May 1949	192,271	58,547	250,818	19,366	8,352	27,718	9.0
June 1949	182,723	57,602	240,325	18,451	8,094	26,545	9.1
July 1949	201,532	51,558	253,090	20,488	7,104	27,592	9.2
August 1949	55,940	21,819	77,759	5,886	3,098	8,984	8.7
September 1949	12,047	4,104	16,151	1,434	551	1,985	8.1
Totals	1,783,573	542,081	2,325,654	189,963	87,719	277,682	8.4
%	77%	23%		68%	32%		
Avg	111,473	33,880	145,353	11,873	5,482	17,355	

* British flights include civilian contractors.

In Bound Cargo									
	Food	%	Coal	%	Other	%	Total	%
US	296,319	55%	1,421,119	90%	66,135	48%	1,783,573	77%
UK	240,528	45%	164,911	10%	136,640	52%	542,079	23%
Total	536,847		1,586,030		202,775		2,325,652	
	23%		68%		9%			

French flights supplying their garrison are not included. They amounted to 800 metric tons (882 US short tons)

US Airlift Cost Split	
$ Cost Area	%
Fuel and Lubricants	21.07%
Field Aircraft Maintenance	4.34%
Administrative Overhead	10.30%
Depreciation and Depot Maintenance	28.72%

Flight Service	4.17%
Automotive Vehicles	2.09%
Subsistence and Undistributed Charges	9.11%
Air Installations and Construction Costs	2.51%
Flight Maintenance	6.35%
Flight Personnel	11.34%

(USAFE 'Berlin Airlift')

Appendix 2: Order of Battle

US

US Military Governors of Germany

Name	Rank	Branch	Position	Start date	End date
Dwight D. Eisenhower	General of the Army	US Army	Governor	8 May 1945	10 November 1945
George S. Patton	General	US Army	Acting Governor	11 November 1945	25 November 1945
Joseph T. McNarney	General	US Army	Governor	26 November 1945	5 January 1947
Lucius D. Clay	General	US Army	Governor	6 January 1947	14 May 1949
Clarence R. Huebner	Lieutenant General	US Army	Acting Governor	15 May 1949	21 September 1949
John J. McCloy		Civilian	High Commissioner	21 September 1949	1 August 1952

USAF Command Organisations
United States Air Force Europe (USAFE) Commanders

Formed from the 8th Air Force in August 1945, moving to Lindsey Air Station, Wiesbaden in September 1945, remaining there until 1973, when the command moved to Ramstein Air Base.

Lieutenant General John K. Cannon	1945 – 1946
Lieutenant General Idwal H. Edwards	1946 – 1947
Lieutenant General Curtis E. LeMay	1947 – 1948
Lieutenant General John K. Cannon	1948 – 1951

US Military Air Transport Service (MATS)[2]	Established 1 June 1948, Andrew's AFB, Maryland	Major General Laurence S Kuter, Commander Rear Admiral John P. Whitney, Vice Commander
USAFE Berlin Airlift Operation	Established 29 June 1948	Brigadier General Joseph Smith, USAFE, Commander
Airlift Task Force (Provisional)	Established 30 July 1948	Major General William H. Tunner, MATS, Commander
Combined Airlift Task Force (CALTF)	Established 15 October 1948 at Wiesbaden	Major General William H. Tunner, MATS, Commander Air Commodore J.W.F. Merer, RAF, Deputy Commander
USAF 1st Airlift Task Force (1st ALTF)	Established 4 November 1948	Major General William H. Tunner, MATS, Commander

US Army European Command (EUCOM)[3]

General of the Army Dwight D. Eisenhower	16 January 1944 – 26 November 1945
General Joseph T. McNarney	26 November 1945 – 15 March 1947
General Lucius D. Clay	15 March 1947 – 15 May 1949
Lieutenant General Clarence R. Huebner	15 May 1949 – 2 September 1949
General Thomas T. Handy	2 September 1949 – 12 August 1952

US Contributing Units

US Army Support Units	
38th Labor Supervision Company	8512nd Labor Service Company (Polish)
4060th Labor Service Company (Lithuanian)	4041st Labor Service Company (Polish)
8958th Labor Service Company (Polish)	66th Heavy Transportation Truck Company
2958th Labor Service Company (German)	67th Heavy Transportation Truck Company
8957th Labor Service Company (German)	559th Ordnance Maintenance Company Wiesbaden, vehicle repair
4052nd Labor Service Company (German)	Quartermaster Corps
4543rd Labor Service Company (Polish)	Transportation Corps
7441st Labor Service Company (German)	**USAF Support Units**
2905th Labor Service Company (German)	7169th Weather Reconnaissance Squadron (Wiesbaden)
	5th Airways and Air Communications Service (AACS)

USAF Military Strength of assigned and attached personnel (CALTF numbers)

Date	Officers	Airmen	Total
September 1948	1,320	3,605	4,925
January 1949	2,374	7,563	9,937
June 1949	2,463	9,017	11,480

(Tunner, 'Report on the Berlin Airlift')

USAF Airlift Structure

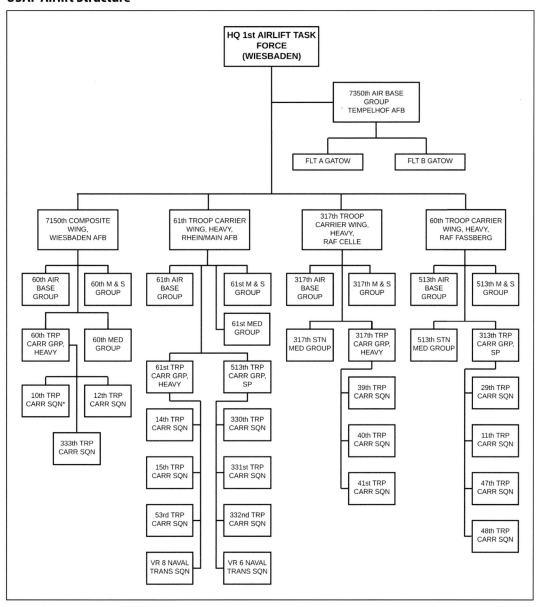

- AFB – Air Force Base
- FLT – Flight
- M and S – Maintenance and Supply
- TRP – Troop
- CARR – Carrier
- MED – Medical
- SQN – Squadron
- SP – Support
- TRANS – Transport
- STN – Station
- * 10th Troop Carrier Squadron –
- not manned
- (USAFE, 'Berlin Airlift')

UK

British Command Organisations
British Military Governor, Control Commission Germany (British Element)

Field Marshal Bernard Law Montgomery	22 May 1945 – 30 April 1946
Air Chief Marshall Sir William Sholto Douglas	1 May 1946 – 31 October 1947
General Sir Brian Robertson	1 November 1947 – 21 September 1949
General Sir Brian Robertson (as High Commissioner)	21 September 1949 – 24 June 1950

CCG (BE) Public Safety Branch Organisation Chart[4]

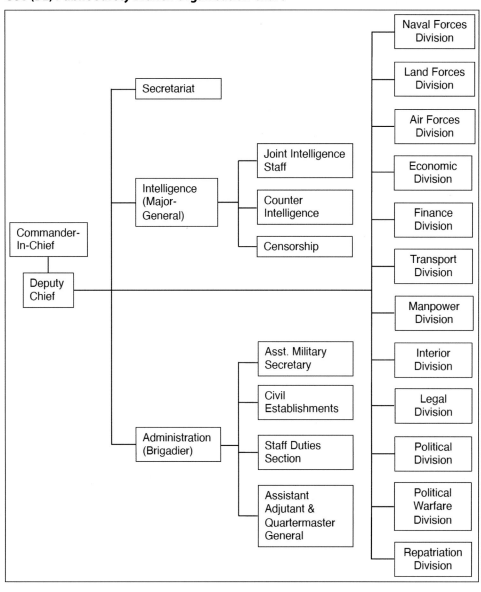

- The Commander-In-Chief was also the British member of the Allied Control Council.
- The Deputy Chief was also the British member of the Coordinating Committee.
- The Public Safety Branch, responsible for civil policing, was in the Interior Division. It had separate sections for CID, Special Branch, Fire Services and Intelligence.

Commandants of the British sector of Berlin

Established in 1945 with headquarters located at Lancaster House, Fehrbelliner Platz, Wilmersdorf, Berlin.

Major General Lewis Lyne	5 July 1945 – 30 August 1945
Maj Gen Eric Nares	30 August 1945 – 13 June 1947
Lieutenant General Sir Otway Herbert	13 June 1947 – 23 January 1949
General Geoffrey Bourne	23 January 1949 – 24 October 1951

British Air Forces of Occupation[5]

Established 15 July 1945 with Headquarters at Bad Eilsen

Commanders in Chief	
Air Chief Marshal Sir Sholto Douglas	15 July 1945 – 1 February 1946
Air Marshal Sir Philip Wigglesworth	1 February 1946 – 30 October 1948
Air Marshal Sir Thomas Williams	30 October 1948 – 1 October 1951

Combined Airlift Task Force (CALTF)

Established 15 October 1948 at Wiesbaden.
Major General William H. Tunner, MATS, USAF, Commander
Air Commodore J.W.F. Merer, RAF, Deputy Commander

RAF Transport Command

Established in March 1943

Commanders in Chief	
Air Marshal Sir Ralph Cochrane	15 February 1945 – 24 September 1947
Air Marshal Sir Brian Baker	24 September 1947 – 31 March 1950

Participating RAF Units

46 Group	Based at Bückeberg. Moved to Lüneburg in March 1949. C-in-C AOC Air Commodore J.W.F. Merer
38 Group	Training Squadrons
Airlift Staff Committee, Berlin	
RAF Berlin Control Zone	Task Force Approach Control
BAFO Air Traffic Control Centre	Bad Eilsen
Nos. 4, 5 and 11 GCA Units	

Participating RAF Stations

RAF Bückeburg	Lower Saxony, Germany
RAF Celle	Lower Saxony, Germany
RAF Faßberg	Lower Saxony, Germany
RAF Gatow	West Berlin
RAF Lübeck	Schleswig-Holstein, Germany
RAF Schleswigland	Schleswig-Holstein, Germany
RAF Wunstorf	Hannover, Germany

N.B. Finkenwerder was not an RAF Station but Sunderland flying boats were operated from there with very basic ground facilities. Fuhlsbüttel was a civilian airport from which British civilian contractors operated.

Participating RAF Squadrons

Squadron	Aircraft type	Notes
10	Douglas Dakota	Renumbered from 238 Squadron in October 1948
18	Douglas Dakota	
24	Douglas Dakota	
27	Douglas Dakota	
30	Douglas Dakota	
46	Douglas Dakota	
53	Douglas Dakota	Dakota Squadron until 1 August 1949 when it became a Hastings Squadron
62	Douglas Dakota	
77	Douglas Dakota	
238	Douglas Dakota	Renumbered to 10 Squadron in October 1948
240 OCU	Douglas Dakota	Operational Conversion Unit
114 (MEDME Det)	Douglas Dakota	MEDME – RAF Mediterranean and Middle East Command
24 (Commonwealth)	Douglas Dakota	24 (Commonwealth) Squadron, comprising ten Dakota crews from Royal Australian Air Force (RAAF), ten Dakota crews from South African Air Force (SAAF) and three Dakota crews from Royal New Zealand Air Force (RNAZF)
40	Avro York	
49	Avro York	
50	Avro York	
51	Avro York	

Squadron	Aircraft type	Notes
59	Avro York	
99	Avro York	
206	Avro York	
241 OCU	Avro York	
242	Avro York	
511	Avro York	511 Squadron operated Yorks until September 1949 and then operated Hastings
47	Handley Page Hastings	
295	Handley Page Hastings	
53	Handley Page Hastings	
297	Handley Page Hastings	
511	Handley Page Hastings	511 Squadron operated Yorks until September 1949 and then operated Hastings
201	Short Sunderland	
230	Short Sunderland	
235 OCU	Short Sunderland	

Combined Airlift Task Force (CALTF) Structure[6]

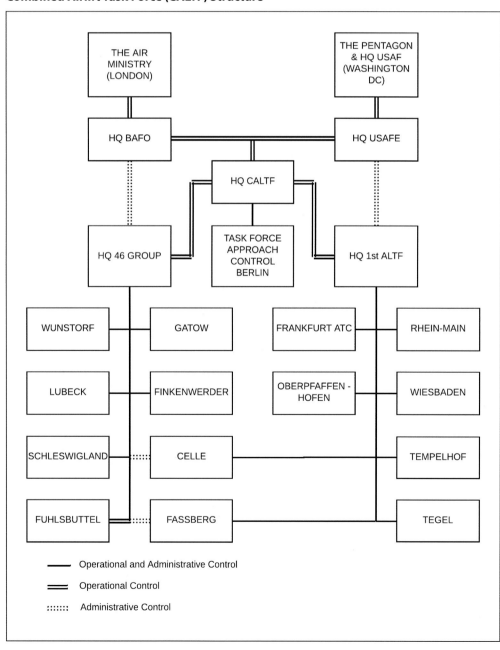

Notes
BAFO – British Air Forces of Occupation
USAF – United States Air Force
USAFE – United States Air Force Europe
CALTF – Combined Air Lift Task Force
ALTF – Air Lift Task Force
Faßberg and Celle – British bases, but US aircraft

Contributing British Army Units

Royal Army Service Corps	British Army Transport Organisation
Royal Engineers	British Army Transport Organisation
Royal Army Service Corps RASO	Rear Airfield Supply Organisation at Wunstorf
Royal Army Service Corps FASO	Forward Airfield Supply Organisation at Gatow
Royal Corps of Signals	Air Formation Unit

Civilian Contractors[7]

Operator	Comment
Air Contractors	Dakotas
Airflight Ltd	Run by AVM Donald Bennett, two Avro Tudors (one freight, one tanker) and a Lincoln tanker
Airwork	Maintenance services and two Bristol Freighters
Air Transport (Channel Islands)	One Dakota
Aquila Airways	Three Short Hythe flying boats
BAAS	British American Air Services, three Halton tankers
BEA	Technical advice and coordination
BNAS	British Nederland Air Services, one Dakota
BSAA	British South American Airways, seven Tudor tankers
BOAC	British Overseas Airways Corporation, three Dakotas
Bond Air Services	12 Handley Page Haltons supplied by Freddie Laker's Aviation Traders
Ciro's Aviation	Two Dakotas belonging to a London nightclub owner, formerly used to ferry wealthy patrons to the French Riviera
Eagle Aviation	Four Handley Page Haltons
Field Aircraft Services	Maintenance
Flight Refuelling Ltd	12 Lancastrian tankers
Hornton Airways	One Dakota
Kearsley Airways	Two Dakotas
Lancashire Aircraft Corporation	13 Halton tankers
Marshalls	Maintenance
Scottish Airlines	Three Liberators as tankers, and two Dakotas
Scottish Aviation	Maintenance
Silver City Airways	Two Bristol Freighters and two Wayfarers
Sivewright Airways	One Dakota
Skyflight	Two Halton tankers
Skyways Ltd	Three Yorks and five Lancastrians
Transworld Charter	Two Vikings
Trent Valley Aviation	One Dakota
Westminster Airways	Two Dakotas and four Haltons
World Air Freight	Three Haltons

Selected Bibliography/Further Reading

Books/Reports

Anon., *Royal Air Force in Germany 1945-1993* (London: Royal Air Force Historical Society, 1999)

Beevor, Antony, *Berlin: The Downfall 1945* (London: Viking Penguin, 2007)

Boyn, Oliver, *The Divided Berlin 1945-1990, The Historical Guidebook* (Berlin: Christoph Links, 2011)

Cannon, Lt. Gen. John K., *Berlin Airlift, A USAFE Summary* (New York: Headquarters United States Air Forces in Europe, 1949)

Collier, Richard, *Bridge Across the Sky, The Berlin Blockade and Airlift, 1948-1949* (USA: McGraw-Hill Book Company, 1978)

Dimbleby, David, *The Battle for the Atlantic* (London: Viking, 2015)

Giangreco, D.M., and Griffin, Robert E., *Airbridge to Berlin – The Berlin Crisis of 1948, its Origins and Aftermath* (USA: Presidio Press, 1988)

Grehan, John, *The Berlin Airlift, The world's largest ever air supply operation* (Barnsley: Air World Books/Pen and Sword Ltd, 2019)

Harrington, Daniel F., *The Air Force Can Deliver Anything, A History of the Berlin Airlift* (USA: United States Air Force, 2008)

Howley, Brig. Gen. Frank L., *A Four Year Report, Office of Military Government, Berlin Sector, July 1, 1945 – September 1, 1949* (Berlin: Public Relations and Historical Branch, Office of Military Government, Berlin Sector, 1949)

Jackson, Robert, *The Berlin Airlift* (Wellingborough: Patrick Stephens, 1988)

Kempe, Frederick, *Berlin 1961* (USA: Penguin, 2011)

Miller, Roger G., *To Save a City, The Berlin Airlift 1948-1949* (USA: Air Force History and Museums Program, 1998)

Slaveski, Filip, *The Soviet Occupation of Germany, Hunger, Mass Violence, and the Struggle for Peace, 1945–1947* (Cambridge: Cambridge University Press, 2013)

Stangl, Paul, *Risen from Ruins – The Cultural Politics of Rebuilding East Berlin* (USA: Stanford University Press, April 2018)

Stivers, William, and Carter, Donald A., *The City Becomes a Symbol, The U.S. Army in the Occupation of Berlin, 1945–1949* (Washington, D.C.: Center of Military History, United States Army, 2017)

Sutherland, Jon and Canwell, Diane, *Berlin Airlift: The Salvation of a City* (Barnsley: Pen and Sword Aviation, 2007)

Taylor, Frederick, *The Berlin Wall, 13 August 1961 – 9 November 1989* (London: Bloomsbury, 2006)

Tunner, Maj Gen William H., *A Report on the Airlift Berlin Mission, the operational and internal aspects of the advance element* (Maxwell AFB, Ala.: Headquarters, Combined Airlift Task Force, 30 August 1949)

Tunner, William H., *Over the Hump* (New York: Duell, Sloan and Pearce, 1964)

Turner, Barry, *The Berlin Airlift, the Relief Operation that Defined the Cold War* (London: Icon Books, 2017)

Journals/Articles

Anon., 'The Evolution of the Bizonal Organization', *Civil Administration Division, Government Structures Branch, Office of Military Government for Germany (US), OMGUS* (March 1948)

Kennan, George, 'Telegram to US Secretary of State, George Marshall 22 February 1946' a.k.a. 'The Long Telegram', *History and Public Policy Program Digital Archive, National Archives and Records Administration, Department of State Records (Record Group 59), Central Decimal File, 1945-1949, 861.00/2-2246; reprinted in US Department of State, ed., Foreign Relations of the United States, 1946, Volume VI, Eastern Europe; The Soviet Union (Washington, DC: United States Government Printing Office, 1969)* (22 February 1946), pp.696-709

Kristensen, Hans M. and Norris, Robert S., 'Global nuclear weapons inventories, 1945–2013', *Bulletin of the Atomic Scientists* (2013)

Provan, Dr. John, 'The Berlin Blockade and Airlift, a Chronology', *Luftbrücke (Airlift) Frankfurt – Berlin 1948-1949 eV c/o Stiftung Luftbrückendank (Airlift Gratitude Foundation)*, (Undated).

Tarnoff, Curt, 'The Marshall Plan: Design, Accomplishments, and Significance', *Congressional Research Service* (18 January 2018)

X (George Kennan), 'The sources of Soviet conduct', *Foreign Affairs. An American Quarterly Review, No 4; Vol. 25, Council of Foreign Affairs, New York* (July 1947) pp.566-582.

Young, John W., 'The Foreign Office, the French and the Post-War Division of Germany 1945-46', *Review of International Studies*, Volume 12, No. 3 (1986), pp.223-34. http://www.jstor.org/stable/20097083.

Useful Websites

Airlift Foundation (Airlift Gratitude Foundation) <www.stiftung-luftbrueckendank.de>

Allied Museum, Berlin <www.alliiertenmuseum.de>

Atomic Archive <www.atomicarchive.com>

Avalon Project, Documents in Law, History and Diplomacy, Yale Law School <avalon.law.yale.edu>

British Berlin Airlift Association <www.bbaa-airlift.org.uk>

CVCE, Centre Virtuel de la Connaissance sur l'Europe (CVCE) @ University of Luxembourg <www.cvce.eu>

George C. Marshall Foundation <www.marshallfoundation.org>

German History in Documents and Images @ The German Historical Society, Washington DC <www.ghdi.ghi-dc.org>

GOV.UK, History of Government, Foreign Affairs and Diplomacy, What's the Context Series <https://history.blog.gov.uk/category/foreign-affairs-and-diplomacy/whats-the-context-series/>

Harry S. Truman Presidential Library and Museum <www.trumanlibrary.gov>

Imperial War Museum <www.iwm.org.uk>

International Churchill Society <www.winstonchurchill.org>

Michigan State University Seventeen Moments in Soviet History <soviethistory.msu.edu>

National Cold War Museum (RAF Museum Cosford) <www.nationalcoldwarexhibition.org>

North Atlantic Treaty Organization, NATO <www.nato.int>

RAF Museum <www.rafmuseum.org.uk>

US State Department, Office of the Historian <https://history.state.gov>.

United States Air Force <www.af.mil> and <www.afhistory.af.mil>

United Nations <www.un.org>

United States Library of Congress <www.loc.gov>

United States National Archives <www.archives.gov> and <www.ourdocuments.gov>

Notes

Introduction

1 Churchill was misquoting American philosopher George Santayana, who said 'Those who cannot remember the past are condemned to repeat it'.

Chapter 1

1 John W Wheeler-Bennett, 'The Meaning of Brest-Litovsk Today'. *Foreign Affairs*, vol. 17, no. 1, 1938, pp.137–152, www.jstor.org/stable/20028909.

2 Although the severity of the 1919 Treaty of Versailles was blamed for the rise of Hitler and the Second World War, the Brest-Litovsk treaty was far harsher in territorial and material terms.

3 Germany finally settled its Versailles reparations obligations on 3 October 2010, which coincided with the 20th anniversary of re-unification. Matters had been complicated by the Second World War and the subsequent division of Germany in the Cold War, but a 1953 agreement settled the terms which concluded with a final interest payment of less than $100 million in 2010.

4 Stalin would eventually succeed in building his Iron Curtain all the way from Poland and the Baltic Sea in the north to Bulgaria and the Black Sea in the south. He was thwarted in his attempt to reach all the way down to the Mediterranean after the Yugoslav-Soviet split in 1948 and after Greece and Turkey were invited to join NATO in 1951. However, the Soviet satellite states forming the buffer would last until the fall of the communist world in 1989-1991. The terms 'Iron Curtain' and 'Special Relationship' were first used by Winston Churchill in his famous speech at Fulton, Missouri on 5 March 1946.

5 The COMINTERN was founded at a Congress held in Moscow on 2–6 March 1919.

6 <https://www.cfr.org/blog/twe-remembers-destroyers-bases-deal> and <https://usnhistory.navylive.dodlive.mil/2014/09/02/destroyers-for-bases-roosevelt-finds-loophole-in-neutrality-act-to-help-great-britain/> both accessed 30 November 2020.

7 Lend Lease Bill, dated January 10, 1941. Records of the U.S. House of Representatives, HR 77A-D13, Record Group 233, National Archives and Records Administration <www.ourdocuments.gov> accessed 30 November 2020.

8 'Agreement Between the United Kingdom and the Union of Soviet Socialist Republics: July 12, 1941', *Department of State Bulletin, September 27, 1941* (Washington DC: Government Printing Office, 1941) <https://avalon.law.yale.edu/wwii/brsov41.asp> accessed 30 November 2020.

9 The Placentia Bay Conference was held on board USS *August*, which was anchored in Placentia Bay, Newfoundland, in Argentia Harbour close to the US Naval base. The joint statement from the two leaders was issued on 14 August 1941.

10 The Atlantic Charter <https://www.nato.int/cps/en/natohq/official_texts_16912.htm> accessed 30 November 2020.

11 The US formal declaration of war on Japan took place the following day, 8 December 1941.

12 United Nations <https://www.un.org/en/sections/history-united-nations-charter/1942-declaration-united-nations/index.html> accessed 30 November 2020.

13 International Churchill Society, 'Coalitions summits 1941-1945, the Wartime Conferences' <https://winstonchurchill.org/publications/finest-hour/finest-hour-147/coalitions-summits-1941-1945-the-wartime-conferences/> accessed 30 November 2020.

14 Churchill famously carved up Eastern Europe on a scrap of paper in a private meeting with Stalin at the Second Moscow Conference (Tolstoy) in October 1944 (a.k.a. Churchill's 'Naughty Document').

15 Office of the Historian, Foreign Service Institute, United States Department of State <https://history.state.gov/historicaldocuments/frus1945v03/d380> and Bruce Kuklick, "The Genesis of the European Advisory Commission." *Journal of Contemporary History, vol. 4, no. 4* (1969), pp.189–201, <www.jstor.org/stable/259844> both accessed 30 November 2020.

16 The Yalta Declaration, The Library of Congress <https://www.loc.gov/law/help/us-treaties/bevans/m-ust000003-1020.pdf> accessed 30 November 2020.

17 Pogue, Forrest C., 'Why Eisenhower's forces stopped at the Elbe', *World Politics, Cambridge University Press* Vol 4, No. 3, (April 1952), pp.356-368.

18 The Miller Centre <https://millercenter.org/president/fdroosevelt/death-of-the-president> accessed 30 November 2020.

19 Joseph Stalin, Winston S. Churchill, Clement R. Attlee, *Correspondence between the Chairman of the Council of Ministers of the USSR and the Presidents of the USA and the Prime Ministers of Great Britain during the Great Patriotic War of 1941-1945, Volume 1, Correspondence with and (July 1941-November 1945)* (Moscow: Progress Publishers 1957), Document No.450, pp.343-344. N.B. the translation from English to Russian and then back to English changes the wording slightly, but the strong message remains: '*There is not much comfort in looking into a future where you and the countries you dominate, plus the Communist parties in many other States, are all drawn up on one side, and those who rally to the English-speaking nations and their Associates or Dominions are on the other. It is quite obvious that their quarrel would tear the world to pieces and that all of us leading men on either side who had anything to do with that would be shamed before history*'.

Chapter 2

1 Treaties and Other International Agreements of the United States of America 1776-1949, compiled under the direction of Charles I. Bevans LL.B., Assistant Legal Advisor Department of State, Volume 3 Multilateral 1931-1945, Department of State Publication 8484 (Washington, DC: Government Printing Office, 1969) <http://avalon.law.yale.edu/wwii/ger01.asp> accessed 30 November 2020

2 Paul Stangl, *Risen from Ruins – The Cultural Politics of Rebuilding East Berlin* (USA: Stanford University Press, April 2018)

3 The SMA had around 40,000 staff by the end of 1945, compared to 1.5 million troops.

4 Beevor, Antony, *Berlin: The Downfall 1945* (London: Viking Penguin, 2007) and <https://www.theguardian.com/books/2002/may/01/news.features11> accessed 30 November 2020

5 Stalin was doing much the same across the other side of the world in Manchuria at the same time.

6 Deutscher Bundestag, 'The political parties in the Weimar Republic', *Administration of the Deutscher Bundestag, Research Section WD 1*, Berlin (March 2006).

7 Walter Ulbricht was born in Leipzig on 30 June 1893 and died 1 August 1973, aged 80.

8 Wilhelm Pieck was born 3 January 1876 and died 7 September 1960, aged 84.

9 Erich Honecker was born 25 August 1912 and died 29 May 1994, aged 81.

10 As related by Wolfgang Leonhard, original member of the Ulbricht Group, who defected from the Soviet Zone in 1949 just before it became the DDR, in his 1955 book Child of the Revolution

11 Zhukov was replaced as head of the SMA by Marshall Vasily Sokolovsky in 1946.

12 PUR was established in May 1919 to supervise the political Commissars and keep control of the Red Army.

13 Bezarin was killed in a motorbike accident on 16 June and was replaced by General Gorbatov.

14 Ivan Serov would go on to become the head of the KGB in 1954 and then head of the GRU in 1958.

15 Abandoned Berlin <https://www.abandonedberlin.com/category/military/soviet-military/> accessed 30 November 2020.

16 United Nations <https://www.un.org/en/sections/history-united-nations-charter/1945-san-francisco-conference/> accessed 30 November 2020.

17 Lancaster House (Fehrbelliner Platz 4) was formerly the offices of the Deutschen Arbeitsfront (German Labour Front), the Nazi equivalent of the trade union movement. Other buildings in the vicinity were used by the SS.

18 Jonathan Walker, *Operation Unthinkable, the Third World War, British Plans to Attack the Soviet Empire 1945* (Stroud; The History Press 2013).

19 Office of the Historian, Foreign Service Institute, United States Department of State <https://history.state.gov/milestones/1937-1945/potsdam-conf> accessed 30 November 2020.

20 Imperial War Museum <https://www.iwm.org.uk/history/how-winston-churchill-and-the-conservative-party-lost-the-1945-election> accessed 30 November 2020.

21 Office of the Historian, Foreign Service Institute, United States Department of State <https://history.state.gov/departmenthistory/people/byrnes-james-francis> accessed 30 November 2020.

22 The Cecilienhof Palace was built between 1913-1917 in a mock-Tudor style for the last of the Hohenzollern dynasty, Crown Prince William of Prussia and his wife Cecile (hence Cecilienhof). Kaiser Wilhelm II (Kaiser Bill) abdicated after the First World War but his family were given special permission to remain in the palace, which they did until 1945.

23 UNESCO World Heritage <https://visitworldheritage.com/en/eu/cecilienhof-palace-in-the-new-garden/4e8e31d3-7819-413f-a4ea-62f06fee36d1> accessed 30 November 2020.

24 A Decade of American Foreign Policy: Basic Documents, 1941-49 prepared at the request of the Senate Committee on Foreign Relations by the Staff of the Committee and the Department of State (Washington, DC: Government Printing Office, 1950), Yale Law School <http://avalon.law.yale.edu/20th_century/decade17.asp>, and Imperial War Museum <https://www.iwm.org.uk/history/how-the-potsdam-conference-shaped-the-future-of-post-war-europe> both accessed 30 November 2020.

25 Although hostilities ended in 1945, the 'Peace Treaty' to officially end Germany's part in the Second World War remained unresolved because of the breakdown of relations between East and West that accompanied the Cold War. Stalin repeatedly threatened to negotiate a separate treaty with East Germany (his puppet state), thus putting the status of West Berlin in jeopardy, but the issue outlasted the Cold War, and almost the Soviet Union, being resolved by the 'Treaty on the Final Settlement with respect to Germany', signed in Moscow on 12 September 1990 in the run up to German reunification.

26 The Trinity Test on 16 July 1945 heralded the start of the Atomic Era and was the end result of years of research by the Manhattan Project. The 'Gadget' was detonated at 5.30am at the Alamogordo Bombing and Gunnery Range in the Jornada Del Muerto Desert, 230 miles south of Los Alamos, resulting in an explosion calculated at 21 kilotons, the equivalent of 21,000 tons of TNT.

27 The Manhattan Project was so secret that even Truman, as Vice President, was not told about it.

28 United States-Department of State. Documents on Germany 1944-1985. Washington: Department of State, [s.d.]. 1421 p. (Department of State Publication 9446). p. 44-48., c/o Centre Virtuel de la Connaissance sur l'Europe (CVCE) @ University of Luxembourg. <https://www.cvce.eu/content/publication/1999/1/1/40dda3a5-d0d1-4496-848d-c0f84309ae8b/publishable_en.pdf> accessed 30 November 2020.

29 The occupation of Manchukuo would last until May 1946 and involved the removal of an estimated $2 billion of war booty by way of reparations as well as the installation of communist-friendly officials. It would also indirectly lead to the arbitrary division of the Korean peninsula along the 38th Parallel North, the creation of Mao Zedong's communist People's Republic of China (PRC) in 1949 and the Korean War in 1950. Truman and his Secretary of State General George Marshall would both be criticised for not intervening in the region and 'allowing' the communists to have free rein, of 'giving away' China.

30 The Japanese Emperor announced the Empire's capitulation over the radio on 15 August 1945, which was the first time most of his subjects had ever heard his voice. The formal surrender ceremony took place on 2 September 1945, on board USS Missouri.

31 There was never any doubt that Stalin would be re-elected – he even had his own electoral 'precinct' in Central Moscow, but the Party wanted to maintain a veneer of democratic process for the faithful and the international media.

32 International Churchill Society <https://winstonchurchill.org/resources/speeches/1946-1963-elder-statesman/the-sinews-of-peace/> accessed 29 November 2020.

33 Churchill's prediction in his letter to Stalin on 28 April 1945 was coming to pass.

34 International Churchill Society <https://winstonchurchill.org/resources/speeches/1946-1963-elder-statesman/the-sinews-of-peace/> accessed 29 November 2020.

Chapter 3

1 The SPD in the West finally received official sanction in January 1946.

2 Adenauer would go on to become the first Chancellor of West Germany in September 1949.

3 Later, the bloc was extended to include the Democratic Peasants' Party of Germany (Demokratische Bauern partei Deutschlands or DBD) which was intended to unite the farming community ahead of the planned collectivisation of agriculture and the National Democratic Party of Germany (National-Demokratische Partei Deutschlands or NDPD), which was formed to accommodate the right-wing including war veterans and former members of the Nazi party.

4 Michael Reschke, Christian Krell, Jochen Dahm (eds), 'History of Social Democracy, Social Democracy Readers', Academy for Social Democracy, Friedrich Ebert-Stiftung (Berlin: September 2013).

5 Other post-war party sponsored newspapers in the Soviet Zone such as Sozialistische Einheit (Socialist Unity) and Vorwärts-Berliner Volksblatt (Berlin People's Gazette) were quickly subsumed into the official 'organ' of the SED.

6 With a 92 percent turnout, the SPD won 48.7 percent, the CDU 22.2, the SED only 19.8 percent and the LDPD 9.3 percent. <https://www.wahlen-berlin.de/Historie/wahldatenbank/Tabellen/1946agh2p.asp> accessed 30 November 2020.

7 An article in the city's Four-Power constitution required a unanimous decision of the Kommandatura to hire or fire officials. The Soviets had filled the city's administration with 'their' people, and then vetoed any attempts to remove them.

8 Central Intelligence Agency, Militarism in East Germany (Langley: CIA Reading Room, April 1959).

9 The actual numbers of deportees and deaths are very hard to determine, given the chaos in post-war Europe and the closed communist system in the Soviet Union. Various studies were made during the 1950s and 60s and further work has been done since the Soviet era archives have been made available although the estimates vary considerably. Suffice it to say that the misery of the Second World War continued for hundreds of thousands of Germans, some innocent, some guilty, for decades after the fighting ended.

10 In 1954, the British Military Government would move to JHQ (Joint Headquarters) Rheindahlen, situated in Mönchengladbach, North Rhine-Westphalia in the far west of West Germany, north west of Cologne and not far from the Belgian border.

11 The Control Commission Germany (British Element) was disbanded in 1955 following West Germany's independence. The High Commissioners were replaced with Ambassadors.

12 The joint land (Plunder) and air (Varsity) operations took place on the night of 23 and 24 March 1945, successfully crossing the Rhine into Germany.

13 A batman is a soldier assigned to a commissioned officer (or group of officers) as a personal servant. The official term used by the British Army in the First World War was Soldier-Servant, but this was replaced by batman during the inter-war years. In this case, the role was as an assistant, runner or general dogsbody, taking care of the menial tasks thus allowing the officers to concentrate on their jobs. It has nothing to do with the comic book hero.

14 The British Frontier Service went through various iterations: in 1946 the Frontier Control Service replaced the troops who had been guarding the border. In 1949 it became the Frontier Inspection Service, and in 1955, the British Frontier Service. It was disbanded in 1991 after reunification.

15 The Corps of Military Police (CMP) was granted 'Royal' status in 1946, becoming the Corps of Royal Military Police (abbreviated to RMP). They were not called the Royal Corps of Military Police (RCMP) in order to avoid confusion with the Royal Canadian Mounted Police (RCMP).

16 Daniel Cowling, Britain and the Occupation of Germany, 1945-49 (Cambridge: Wolfson College, University of Cambridge, June 2018). Christopher Knowles, Winning the peace: the British in occupied Germany, 1945-1948 (London: King's College London, February 2014). Correlli Barnett, Post-conquest Civil Affairs: Comparing War's End in Iraq and in Germany (London: The Foreign Policy Centre, February 2005). Edward R. Flint, The Development of British Civil Affairs and its Employment in the British Sector of Allied Military Operations during the Battle of Normandy, June to August 1944 (Shrivenham: Cranfield University, September 2008). CCG(BE) and Central Office of Information, Trained to Serve (1948) via Imperial War Museum. CCG (BE), Crown Film Unit and Army Film Unit, A defeated Germany: A film about the Government of the British Occupation of Germany (1946) via Imperial War Museum.

17 US Constabulary <https://history.army.mil/reference/cstb46.htm>, <https://history.army.mil/html/forcestruc/constab-ip.html> and <https://armyhistory.org/mobility-vigilance-justice-the-u-s-constabulary-forces-in-germany-1946-1952/> all accessed 30 November 2020.

18 The Evolution of the Bizonal Organization, Civil Administration Division, Government Structures Branch, (Office of Military Government for Germany (US), OMGUS, March 1948).

19 Yale Law School <https://avalon.law.yale.edu/20th_century/trudoc.asp> and US National Archive and Records Administration <https://www.ourdocuments.gov> both accessed 30 November 2020.

20 Peter Grose, 'The Boss of Occupied Germany: General Lucius D. Clay', Foreign Affairs, 77, no. 4 (1998), pp.179-85. Accessed February 16, 2020. doi:10.2307/20049040.

21 The only Four-Power organisations to stand the test of time in the city was the Berlin Air Safety Centre (BASC), which governed the airspace over Berlin and lasted until re-unification, and Spandau Prison, housing Nazi war crimes prisoners. Spandau closed soon after Rudolf Hess, Hitler's deputy and the last remaining prisoner, committed suicide on 17 August 1987. He had been the sole inmate since 1966 and the building was swiftly demolished in order to stop it becoming a neo-Nazi shrine.

22 Rationing was introduced in the UK in 1940 and would continue until 1954.

23 Signed in December 1945, the loan was on commercial terms and included various sweeteners for the Americans; extended leases on military bases

and access to aviation/telecommunications markets. It was finally paid back in December 2006. Source: Gill Bennett, 'What's the Context? Signing the Anglo-American Financial Agreement, 6 December 1945' (History of Government Blog, UK Government, 7 December 2020) < https://history.blog.gov.uk/2020/12/07/whats-the-context-signing-the-anglo-american-financial-agreement-6-december-1945/> accessed 14 December 2020.

24 The George C. Marshall Foundation <https://www.marshallfoundation.org/marshall/the-marshall-plan/marshall-plan-speech/> accessed 30 November 2020.

25 The Organisation for European Economic Cooperation, OEEC, was the European reciprocal organisation to the American ECA, handling the distribution of aid throughout Europe. Source: Curt Tarnoff, 'The Marshall Plan: Design, Accomplishments, and Significance', *Congressional Research Service, Washington DC* (January 18, 2018).

26 U.S. Agency for International Development (USAID), Bureau for Program and Policy Coordination (November 16, 1971).

27 Millions of dollars were secretly channelled into the blandly titled Office of Policy Coordination (OPC), which was tasked with running US covert operations in Europe to support the political aims of the plan. For example, it established 'front' businesses in several European countries and funded an extensive propaganda campaign which was credited with keeping the communists out of power in the 1948 Italian elections. The OPC was merged with other departments within the CIA in 1952.

28 One fact that Stalin would prefer hidden from the US was the estimated 15-20,000 American former prisoners of war who had been 'liberated' by the advancing Red Army. Along with colleagues from the Korean and Vietnam wars, these American nationals disappeared into the Soviet Gulag system, never to emerge. After the Soviet empire collapsed in the early 1990s, attempts were made to trace them, but the situation still remains largely unresolved.

29 Scott D. Parrish and Mikhail M. Narinsky, 'New evidence on the Soviet Rejection of the Marshall Plan 1947', *Cold War International History Project, Working Paper No. 9* (Washington D.C., Woodrow Wilson International Centre for Scholars, 1994).

Chapter 4

1 Office of the Historian, Foreign Service Institute, United States Department of State, <https://history.state.gov/historicaldocuments/frus1948v02/d210> accessed 30 November 2020.

2 OMGUS – Office of Military Government, United States – the press conference was scheduled for after the banks had all closed for business, not opening again until the following Monday morning.

3 D.M. Giangreco and Robert E.Griffin, *Airbridge to Berlin – The Berlin Crisis of 1948, its Origins and Aftermath* (USA: Presidio Press, 1988).

4 CVCE <http://www.cvce.eu/obj/first_law_on_currency_reform_20_june_1948-en-a5bf33f8-fca0-4234-a4d2-71f71a038765.html> accessed 30 November 2020.

5 The Allies only had around 7,000 troops in the city, outnumbered 3 to 1 by Soviet troops, with many more stationed throughout the Soviet Zone.

6 Maj Gen William H. Tunner, *A Report on the Airlift Berlin Mission, the operational and internal aspects of the advance element* (Maxwell AFB, Ala.: Headquarters, Combined Airlift Task Force, 30 August 1949)

7 The 60th Troop Carrier Group were repositioned to the better location of Wiesbaden on 27 June.

8 A Nissen hut is a prefabricated steel structure used by the military use, especially for barrack accommodation and offices. It was designed during the First World War by the Canadian-British engineer Major Peter Norman Nissen and is made from a half-cylindrical skin of corrugated iron. The American equivalent was called the Quonset hut.

9 Some wags in the British garrison responded to the operation's name by tying underpants to the radio aerials of their vehicles!

10 USAFE, *Berlin Airlift, A USAFE Summary* (New York, Headquarters United States Air Forces in Europe, 1949), pp.109-114 and other sources.

11 The British Berlin Airlift Association <www.bbaa-airlift.org.uk> accessed 30 November 2020.

12 The DUKW (colloquially known as Duck) is a six-wheel-drive amphibious modification of the 2.5 ton CCKW trucks used by the U.S. military during the Second World War.

13 The Tegel site was also earmarked for parachute supply drops, until these were ruled out.

14 The destruction of the tower did not stop the Soviets for long – they began broadcasting soon after from another transmitter in Grünau, close to Schönefeld Airfield in the Soviet sector.

15 In a classic case of Nazi form over function, the marble looked fantastic, but was treacherous when wet.

16 Britain and the Berlin Airlift, *Training Group Media Services, Headquarters Personnel and Training Command, Air Historical Branch* (RAF) (May 1998).

17 In mid-July, the Army Air Transport Organisation moved to Bückeburg, where BAFO was based.

18 The city authority in post-war Berlin was called the Magistrat, following a precedent dating back to 1920s. When the administration split along political lines in November 1948, the Soviet sector civil administration called itself the 'Demokratischen Magistrat' and continued to operate out of the Rotes Rathaus (Red Town Hall) in the Berlin district of Mitte, while the civil administration covering the western sectors moved to Rathaus Schöneberg (Schöneberg Town Hall) in Tempelhof-Schöneberg, calling itself Der Senat von Berlin.

19 The Avro Lincoln was the successor to the famous Lancaster bomber. The B-29 was the bomber that dropped the atomic bombs on Hiroshima and Nagasaki.

20 GI stands for 'General' or 'Government' Issue. The RAF trialled shipping coal in their version of the GI duffel bag – the standard issue white kitbag – which did not stay white for long.

21 The opposite of IFR, Instrument Flight Rules is VFR, Visual Flight Rules, which is based on pilot observation.

22 In an excellent example of how American English differs from British English, 'Big Willie 5678' would mean C-54 number 5678 returning to base, to the sound of tittering from any Brits listening in on the frequency.

23 Aviation Study Manual, Vol 1, Book 2, *US Civil Air Patrol* (August 1949) Section 7, p.79.

24 The opposite of GCA is GCI, Ground Controlled Intercept, where aircraft are guided to an enemy contact by ground-based Radar.

25 Researching Berlin Airlift's statistics is complicated by the different definitions of what a 'ton' is, depending on which side of the Atlantic the source is from and when it was published. An American ton (often called a 'short' ton) is equivalent to 2,000 US pounds. A metric tonne is slightly heavier, equating to 1,000kg, which works out as 2,204.6 American tons. The British ton, a.k.a. the 'long' ton is even heavier, at 2,240 pounds. The British began to adopt the metric system in the late 60s, so contemporary sources are likely to be in short or long tons, depending on whether they are American or British. If this is confusing for the 21st century researcher, and potentially more-so on the ground in Germany in 1948 – the differences caused no end of confusion to planners throughout the supply chain and throughout the airlift. The lessons learnt from the airlift went into the new NATO organisation, where standardisation and interoperability became core elements of their operations. NATO opted for the metric system, but even then, there are numerous exceptions.

26 The British Air Forces of Occupation, BAFO, were set up in 1945. They were re-named as RAF Second Tactical Air Force (2TAF) in 1951 and again as RAF Germany (RAFG) in 1959.

27 The full list of civilian operators is included in the appendices.

28 The Americans struggled with the pronunciation of Oberpfaffenhofen and it became known as Oberhuffinpuffin.

29 Barry Turner, *The Berlin Airlift, the Relief Operation that Defined the Cold War* (London: Icon Books, 2017).

30 Tunner, *Report on the Airlift Berlin Mission.*

31 The Bizonal Economic Council (Wirtschaftsrat) was established on 10 June 1947 and formed post-war Germany's first legislative body, the forerunner to the Bundestag. BICO also ran the sizeable procurement operation, sourcing the various items from all over the world and despatching them to the various distribution hubs in western Germany.

32 At the time, the US Air Force even operated differently from the US Navy, let alone the RAF. NATO was created as a result of the North Atlantic Treaty on 4 April 1949.

33 This incident took place on 5 April 1948 between a Soviet Yak-3 fighter and a British European Airways Vickers Viking, leaving 11 people dead.

34 Public Relations, Statistical and Historical Branch, 'A Four Year Report, July 1, 1945 – September 1, 1949', *Office of Military Government US Sector Berlin* (Berlin 1949) c/o U.S. National Library of Medicine, Bethesda, MD.

35 The 'rent-a-mobs' were mobilised through the FDJ, the Communist Youth Movement run by Erich Honecker. The Bolsheviks had used similar tactics in the Russian parliament in the run up to the October Revolution of 1917.

36 The Platz der Republik would become the venue for some of the big music events held in the run up to the Wall coming down.

37 Reuter was elected Lord Mayor on 27 May 1947, but his appointment was vetoed by the SMA. After a separate West Berlin Assembly was set up in Schöneberg, Reuter was unanimously voted back as Lord Mayor – of West Berlin.

38 'Ihr Völker der Welt ... Schaut auf diese Stadt und erkennt, dass ihr diese Stadt und dieses Volk nicht preisgeben dürft, nicht preisgeben könnt!'

39 Composite sources, reflecting most up to date estimates: USAFE, *Berlin Airlift*, pp.12-13; BAFO, 'A Report on Operation Plainfare (The Berlin Airlift) [AP 3257]' (April 1950) pp.129; USAFE Press Release, n.d., as quoted in Roger Launius and Coy F. Cross, II, *MAC and the Legacy of the Berlin Airlift* (Scott AFB, IL, 1989) pp.58-59; 'Un demi siecle de transport aerien militaire', *Air Actualities* 485 (Sep 95), pp.45. All via Daniel F. Harrington, *The Air Force Can Deliver Anything – a History of the Berlin Airlift* (Ramstein, Germany, 1998 and Langley AFB, VA, 2008).

40 The PX was the Post Exchange (also known as the BX, Base Exchange), the store on a US military base where troops could buy products from home. The British equivalent was the NAAFI.

41 Roberts would go on to be British Ambassador to the Soviet Union and to the Federal Republic of Germany.

42 Richard Collier, *Bridge Across the Sky, The Berlin Blockade and Airlift, 1948-1949* (USA: McGraw-Hill Book Company, 1978).

43 France controversially withdrew from NATO's integrated military command structure in 1966, and while remaining an ally, did not fully re-join until 2009.

44 North Atlantic Treaty Organization NATO <https://www.nato.int/cps/en/natohq/official_texts_17120.htm> accessed 30 November 2020.

45 United States Department of State, Germany 1947-1949: The Story in Documents (Washington DC: U.S. Government Printing Office 1950) pp.88-92.

46 Germany: Removal of Restrictions on Communications, Transportation and Trade (End of Berlin Blockade) (4 May 1949) c/o Library of Congress <https://www.loc.gov/law/help/us-treaties/bevans/m-ust000004-0843.pdf> accessed 30 November 2020.

47 The Basic Law for the Federal Republic of Germany – Grundgesetz für die Bundesrepublik Deutschland.

48 This would eventually happen on 31st August 1990 with the Unification Treaty between the FRG and the GDR, returning the country's capital to Berlin.

49 German History in Documents and Images <https://ghdi.ghi-dc.org/sub_document.cfm?document_id=2858> accessed 30 November 2020.

50 Sixth meeting of Council of Foreign Ministers: German question and Austrian Treaty c/o Library of Congress <https://www.loc.gov/law/help/us-treaties/bevans/m-ust000004-0846.pdf> accessed 30 November 2020.

51 Hans M. Kristensen and Robert S. Norris, 'Global nuclear weapons inventories, 1945–2013', *Bulletin of the Atomic Scientists* (2013), 69:5, pp.75-81.

52 In 1967, the US possessed a staggering 31,255 nuclear weapons.

53 Meyer, Jeffrey, *36th Wing Heritage Pamphlet 1940-1994, 80th Anniversary Issue* (Guam: Andersen AFB, 2019).

Conclusion

1 Office of the Historian, Foreign Service Institute, United States Department of State, <https://history.state.gov/milestones/1945-1952/chinese-rev> accessed 30 November 2020.

Appendices

1 Composite sources, reflecting most up to date estimates: USAFE, *Berlin Airlift*, pp.12-13; BAFO, Report on Operation Plainfare p.129; USAFE Press Release, pp.58-59; Un demi siecle de transport aerien militaire, p.45, via Daniel Harrington, *The Air Force Can Deliver Anything*.

2 Jay H. Smith, *Anything, Anywhere, Anytime: An Illustrated History of the Military Airlift Command 1941-1991* (Scott Air Force Base, Illinois: Office of History, Military Airlift Command, May 1991) pp. 65-68.

3 <https://www.europeafrica.army.mil/Mission-History/> accessed 30 November 2020.

4 Office of The Adjutant General, *Charts showing Organization of Control Commission (British Element)*, 10 November 1944.

5 Royal Air Force Historical Society, *Royal Air Force in Germany, 1945-1993* (Joint Services Command and Staff College, Bracknell, 9 December 1998).

6 USAFE, *Berlin Airlift* p.4 and Tunner, *Report on the Airlift Berlin Mission* pp.17, 18 and 19.

7 Jon Sutherland and Diane Canwell, *Berlin Airlift: The Salvation of a City* (Barnsley: Pen and Sword Aviation, 2007), Robert Jackson, *The Berlin Airlift* (Wellingborough: Patrick Stephens, 1988) and previous sources.

COLD WAR BERLIN: AN ISLAND CITY VOLUME 1 – THE BIRTH OF THE COLD WAR, THE COMMUNIST TAKE-OVER AND THE BERLIN AIRLIFT, 1945 TO 1950

ABOUT THE AUTHOR

Andrew Long, from Great Britain, is a military history researcher and author. His fascination with the Cold War began with a trip to West Berlin in 1986, travelling through Checkpoint Charlie to visit the East. Andrew's writing comes from a desire to make sense of an extremely complex period in modern history, weaving together inter-relating stories involving politics, ideologies, personalities, technological advances and geography. There is still much to be told on this fascinating subject. After a successful career in marketing, Andrew relocated to Cornwall and took up writing full time. This is his first in a series of titles for Helion's @War series on the Cold War.